YANGTZE

EXPLORING THE
YANGTZE
CHINA'S LONGEST RIVER

HOW MAN WONG

CHINA
BOOKS
& Periodicals, Inc.

EXPLORING THE YANGTZE
CHINA'S LONGEST RIVER

© Copyright How Man Wong, 1989

Published by China Books & Periodicals, Inc.,
2929 24th Street, San Francisco, CA 94110,
United States of America

ISBN: 0-8351-2185-2

LFC Imagery (pages 2–3 and 162–5) reproduced
by kind permission of Chicago Aerial Survey Inc., USA

Design and artwork by Joan Law Design & Photography
Printed in Hong Kong

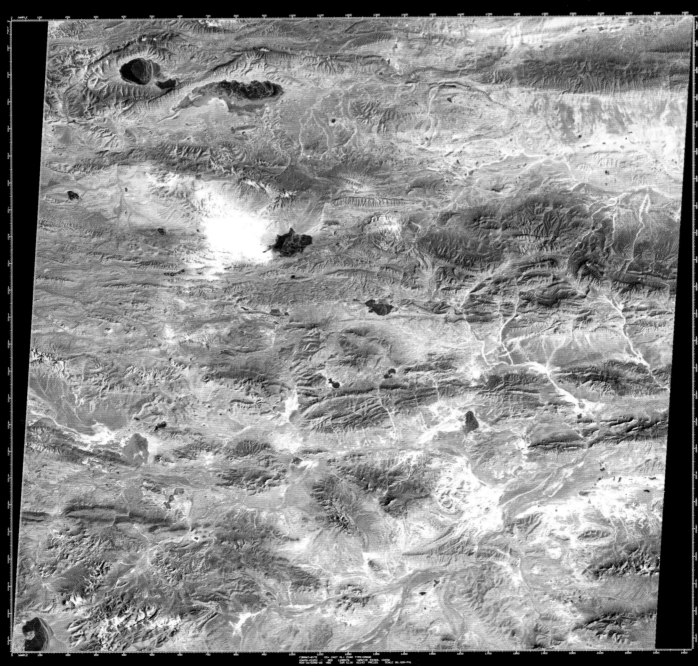

ACKNOWLEDGEMENTS

I would like to extend my sincere gratitude to Wilbur Garrett, Editor, and Mary G Smith, Senior Assistant Editor, at the National Geographic Society. Their support and encouragement made this expedition possible. I would also like to thank the many individuals at the National Geographic who helped in numerous ways in the course of this expedition.

I am indebted to my Tibetan guides on the plateau; without their help and guidance, I would never have made it to the source. They are Bomai, Bola, Nyima Tsering, Yendeng Tsering, Dawa Gongbu, Guodo and Mrude.

I would also like to thank Huang Jingpo, ex-Governor of Qinghai Province, who was instrumental in making our expedition to the source a success. My special thanks also to the following members of the expedition team, Mr Wu Tianfu, my liaison person, traveling companion and Deputy Secretary General of Canton; his wife Huang Waiping; Tan Weiqiang and Wu Weiqiang, my drivers from Canton; Chen Jian, my traveling companion in the lower Yangtze; Jeff Chop and Warren Gee, my American-Chinese assistants; and Marion Fay who accompanied us to the matrilineal villages. There are also scores of individuals and government officials who helped coordinate the long expedition — to all of them I owe a great deal.

Many manufacturers of expedition equipment assisted, or supported our work. Among them Zodiac supplied our inflatable boat; Mariner our outboard motor; Sevylor our canoes; Gregory our backpacks; Marmot our sleeping bags; Northface our tents; O'Neill our drysuits; Honda our off-road motorcycle; Fisher the mountain bikes; Toyota was helpful with our vehicle parts; Tom Cepek of Dick Cepek, Inc. offered invaluable advice on off-road situations, and modifications for our Toyota Landcruiser; Denis Morrison of Northwest Airlines helped with the handling of much of our air transport and cargo. To all of them, I offer my thanks.

I would also like to thank Dr Charles Elachi, Assistant Laboratory Director of the Jet Propulsion Laboratory (NASA/Caltech) for allowing me to use their Shuttle Imaging Radar, Large Format Camera and other remote sensing data; Martin Ruzek at NASA who helped me locate and analyse this data; and Dr Tom Farr at JPL for the acquisition of satellite images. And I would like to thank the Board of Directors and individual members of the China Exploration and Research Society whose untiring support for my work encouraged me to finish this book.

Last, but not least, I thank my parents who taught me at an early age a Chinese proverb which inspired me to pursue this work.

The Landsat MSS is another form of remote-sensing data I used in exploring the upper Yangtze. The frame here covers an area of 180 square kilometers, and was taken from a satellite 920 kilometers above the earth. The image shows the confluence of Tuotuohe and Dam Qu. The lake showing at the lower left-hand corner is Quemoqo. Here our team stopped to take bearings before turning south into the glacial valley and source of the Tuotuohe. Dam Qu's source, or the new source of the Yangtze, is beyond the lower right corner of this image, flowing in a northwesterly direction to join the Tuotuohe, together becoming Tongtianhe. (Scene ID 20659–03353, November 11, 1976, Color Composite Bands 4, 5, and 7 in blue, green and red respectively.)

Page 5
The nomadic camp of Kaxigong is four days on horseback west of Zadoi in southeastern Qinghai. In this basin the two headwaters of the Dam Qu meet. Guangzhugou, in the foreground, is the source of Dam Qu, and is thus considered the source of the Yangtze River. By early September, the plateau here is already experiencing its first snow of the season.

Pages 8-9
Silhouetted against Lake Honghu in Hubei Province, fishermen work over their nets for an early catch. The lake is home to a variety of fish and waterfowl. Draining into the Yangtze, it can be used as a safety valve for flood control during the high-water season.

Pages 10-11
Extensive terracing takes up any arable land in canyons of the middle Yangtze. Once the massive dam is built, the isolated valleys inside the Three Gorges may be altered forever.

Pages 12-13
A yak herd grazes at an altitude of over 5,000 meters near Jianggendiru Glacier which is the source of the Tuotuohe.

CONTENTS

PREFACE

The Yangtze is one of the longest rivers in the world, and without question is the most important river in human terms with over 300 million people — over seven percent of the world's population — living within the confines of its basin. The Yangtze, too, is a major artery of communication in China. It has greatly influenced the course of Chinese history, and continues to inspire poets and painters. Its source has only recently and tentatively been mapped, and I am sure that even today, as Wong How Man has shown, there is much more to be discovered about this mighty river.

The Yangtze has inspired both me and Wong How Man, and has enabled us to realize our own dreams. Mine was to make the first cruise along its navigable length and open up this region to the outside world. Wong How Man's to trace the length of the river all the way to the source.

Over the last 30 years I have been an explorer of sorts myself, pioneering travel to some of the world's most exotic places, from the Seychelles to the Antarctic, from Easter Island to the Gobi Desert. And in the late 1970s, I used the very vessel that had been built for Chairman Mao on Lindblad Travel's inaugural Yangtze River cruise. I shall never forget the excited crowds who greeted us on that trip, as we stopped at towns and villages where few of the people had ever seen a foreigner before. And I can imagine just how exciting it has been for Wong How Man to go into newly discovered areas.

Although our ships have been plying the lower and middle reaches for the last decade, the Yangtze remains relatively untraveled, especially in the regions further upstream. It is these rugged, inaccessible areas, in particular, that Wong How Man has explored and photographed.

As with all the world's major rivers, the upper reaches of the Yangtze are shrouded in mystery. The first reasonably accurate estimate of the river's length was only obtained in 1978, following the first Chinese expedition to find the river's source. From later aerial surveys, and from his own explorations, Wong How Man has discovered a more likely source, which extends the length of the river still more.

The Yangtze is one of the most varied and scenically beautiful of all rivers, and perhaps most famous for the spectacular Three Gorges, historically a hazardous region for navigation. More recently, other remarkable areas have become more widely known such as the spectacular Tiger Leaping Gorge and the forbidding Qinghai-Tibet plateau.

Wong How Man's splendid book will dazzle the world with its portrayal of the scenic wonders of this great river, and the diverse peoples who dwell along its route. The record of his exploration and discoveries, and especially his stunning photographs, will be treasured by those who have already seen the river — and will surely be an inspiration to others.

Lars-Eric Lindblad
President, Lindblad Travel, Inc.

Many of Asia's great rivers have their sources on the Qinghai–Tibet Plateau. This river originates from the Tanggula Range in northern Tibet and feeds the headwaters of the Nu River which flows south through Yunnan into Burma. Nomadic camps dot the landscape of a high summer pasture.

Exploring China's Longest River

'I stood with one foot on each bank of the Yangtze!'

The old man in the Shanghai suburb looks at me as though I were joking. After all, the Yangtze at this point near the estuary is over 30 kilometers wide and, on a day like this we cannot even see the other bank.

Joking I am not. I have just returned from months of exploration at the headwaters of the Yangtze and, at the source of the river, I strode across it with but one step.

In ten months of travel over a two-year period, I came to know this river intimately — her pulse, her temperament, her joys and her sorrows.

As a photojournalist for the National Geographic Society, I was originally invited to participate in a rafting adventure down the upper Yangtze, a river I had been researching for five years. But I realized that river-running wasn't what I wanted to do; what I really desired was to study the full length of the Yangtze and to explore the remote upper reaches of the Tibetan Plateau.

As a child, my parents had continually reminded me of the famous Chinese proverb: 'When drinking water, think about the source.' Perhaps as a consequence of this, I was curious to learn the true source of this magnificent 6,400-kilometer-long river.

When we finally reached the Yangtze's known source, our Tibetan nomad guides verified the speculation of another longer and more important source. With this discovery, we hoped that the Yangtze might come close to, or even surpass, the Amazon in length and be recognized as the second-longest river in the world.

But length alone cannot determine a river's greatness. Its drainage area of 1.8 million square kilometers is one-fifth of the land area of China, and its history and destiny affect one-third of China's billion people that live along its basin. The Yangtze cuts China in half; its flow from the Tibetan highlands in the west to Shanghai and the China Sea in the east neatly divides the Chinese into Northerners and Southerners.

Together with the National Geographic, I developed an ambitious plan to study the full length of the Yangtze by following the trunk river as closely as possible from mouth to source, a feat never before attempted.

Two tons of material and equipment were flown into China in 1985, including a Zodiac inflatable boat with a Mariner 25-horsepower motor, a canoe, an off-road motorcycle, mountain bicycles and a huge assortment of freeze-dried food and camping equipment. In addition, we brought in our own four-wheel-drive Landcruiser. To prepare the vehicle for off-road exploration, in Canton we installed a power winch and all-terrain tires, reinforced the shocks and springs, and added a heavy-duty roof rack. Test-driving it on the streets of the city caused a sensation.

Tan Weiqiang (Shorty) and Wu Weiqiang (Bumpy), similar in name but not personality, were our two drivers from Canton. Jeff Chop and Warren Gee, the two American Chinese in our party, took care of mechanical and medical problems, respectively. The rest of the party expanded or de-

Our party

creased depending on which stretch of the river we were covering, from three to 12 members.

THE LOWER REACHES

We set out from Canton in early March on our drive north to reach the banks of the Yangtze. One of our first stops was the Yangtze Valley Planning Office at Wuhan.

'The Changjiang (Long River) is treacherous and difficult to tame, both for a hydrologist and a boatman,' remarked Cao Le'an, a pre-1949 US graduate and 35-year veteran of the office. His next line: 'Our goal is to put the river to work for the people,' sounded all too familiar in China.

Some hundred kilometers downstream at Xiaogu Shan, an old monk saw it differently: 'The Changjiang is peaceful, like a mirror flowing by, the seated statue on top of this monastery is that of Xiaogu, our guardian goddess who is beautifying herself in front of this mirror,' he said.

That contrast portrays the great river well. When it is peaceful, the Yangtze serves its populace, nourishing a good harvest and providing a granary for almost half the nation's food products. But at other times, its ravaging water inundates thousands of kilometers and leaves devastation behind. The massive flood of 1931 menaced seven provinces, left over 140,000 people dead and made 28 million people homeless. As a farmer along the Yangtze said: 'We can't do without it and we can't deal with too much of it.' It seems to act in accordance with Chinese Yin and Yang cosmology, where an advantage is always checked by a disadvantage, and vice versa.

Jiang Meilong, a 59-year-old chief engineer of the 73rd Engineering and Dike Protection Headquarters at Jiujiang, related their achievements in flood control: 'Twice over the last 35 years, the water level of the Yangtze reached dangerous levels around Jiujiang... once in 1954 and again in 1983. Both times our dikes here survived the test,' Jiang continued, in his distinctive Jiangxi accent, 'though in 1983 the volume of water was less than that of 1954, the level of water was actually higher. Fortunately, we raised the dikes another meter between those years.' I presumed the higher water level must have been because silting had raised the riverbed, but Jiang corrected me: 'Not so! Unlike the past, all the dikes along the Changjiang have been securely reinforced. Since there is no more breaking of dikes further upstream, those of us downstream are faced with a much higher level of water to contain. This kind of achievement upstream can sometimes create another kind of dilemma for us downstream.'

Similar problems were discussed by earlier Chinese hydrologists in their writings. One account by Wang Baixin of the Qing Dynasty has this to say: 'If the left dike is strong, the right dike gets hurt. If both dikes are strong, the lower dikes burst.' Thus he recommended drainage into pre-assigned land as a reservoir and a safety valve.

An old monk, Xiaogu Shan

Height of the 1931 flood

His theory was endorsed in earnest soon after the forming of the People's Republic. The Jinjiang Flood Diversion Project designated some 920 square kilometers of low land as a retention basin should the water of the Yangtze reach a dangerous level. Three years after completion of this project, it effectively lowered the level of the Yangtze near Shashi by one meter during the high waters of 1954.

In a regular year, this huge expanse of land provides some 500,000 hectares of farmland for close to half a million people. While the building of permanent structures is not encouraged by the government, I saw local inhabitants putting up stone houses. I asked Yun Zhongshi why he was doing so. 'It's been 20 years since the last flooding of this area was necessary,' he told me, 'and I am tired of living in flimsy sheds. After all, in the event of an actual diversion flooding, we would be given prior notice to retreat into the 21 safety areas and 100 safety terraces so that human losses would be cut to a minimum. And I am taking this risk willingly.' I only hope the 'prior notice' comes early enough.

Dikes are an all-important part of the river system in the middle and lower Yangtze. For almost 2,000 kilometers, from Yichang to Shanghai, the Yangtze is contained by these man-made embankments. Their role is particularly crucial along the 182-kilometer stretch near Shashi in Hubei Province. Work began on these dikes 16 centuries ago. But some broke so frequently they were nicknamed 'doufu' (beancurd) dikes, by the people.

When early technology failed to contain the Yangtze, people looked for spiritual help. Pagodas were built along the river where flooding usually occurred. In 1788, during the reign of Qianlong of the Qing Dynasty, flooding of the Yangtze inundated over 30 counties in Hubei Province. The emperor ordered nine iron oxen to be cast and put along the Yangtze as

The Jinjiang Flood Diversion Project

One of the many pagodas along the Yangtze

The cabin of a converted junk

The view from behind the dashboard

guardians. The court record explains: 'The Sea Dragon submits to Iron, and the Ox belongs to Earth (based on the Theory of the Five Elements in Chinese cosmology), Earth controls Water, thus the Iron Ox can suppress the flood.'

The city of Shashi and its surrounding plains lay three to seven meters below the surface of the Yangtze during high water. For inhabitants living along the banks, this saying is popular: 'Inside the house you raise your eyes, above your head the boat passes by.'

These passing boats come in all shapes and dimensions. From the ancient junks and sampans to the modern-day fleet of ocean-going liners, from the ultra-simple, single-pole bamboo rafts to the barges with living quarters on top, the Yangtze has them all.

The river is navigable by boats of 15,000 tons to Nanjing, 5,000 tons to Wuhan, 3,000 tons to Yichang, 1,500 tons to Chongqing and 500 tons to Yibin, for a total river distance of almost 3,000 kilometers. Above Yibin, small river boats can ply upstream for another 100 kilometers to Xinshizhen, beyond which only sections of the upper river are navigable, or plied by ferry boats.

In these lower reaches of the Yangtze, we investigated the people whose lives are tied to the river. At Pengze, we boarded a 24-horsepower cargo boat, a converted junk, carrying a load of 65 tons between Shanghai and Wuhan. I held on to the dashboard to stabilize myself as I talked to Captain Qin Yezhong, the owner, on the bridge. Cigarette in mouth, he casually steered his vessel across the choppy water where Puyanghu, China's largest lake, drains into its largest river.

Chart showing tidal changes

As the boat lurched from side to side, the Captain told me: 'The waves are only a couple of meters high, and at this place they really are no big deal.' Qin exhaled another puff, 'It's grade 40, and when it reaches grade 60, then we'll stop.'

I managed to learn that it took him eight days to take his boat to Nanjing and back, a distance of 850 kilometers round trip. If the entire boat is chartered, one way can cost over 3,000 yuan (US$1,000). Charges are based on an intricate combination of tonnage per day, hours of operation, surcharge per horsepower and eight different grades of goods category. Or did he say seven grades? My head got dizzier with each figure.

His story about the water ghosts was more stimulating. As a rule, ghosts and demons are thought to string themselves along behind a boat and proceed on board when the time is ripe to perform their little evils. It is generally believed that by steering one's boat and cutting its stern directly in front of the bow of another boat, the string of ghosts would be cut off and end up on the boat behind. In the past, it was a game which often left the trailing boat's owner jumping, cursing and shooting off firecrackers to pacify his increased string of ghosts.

Among thousands of domestic boats and ships, only a few foreign ones manage to get a short distance into the Yangtze today, unlike a century ago, when foreigners not only controlled the passage of the river, but also the customs houses along its major ports. At the newly finished harbor below Nanjing, I saw a Libyan ship moored in the middle of the Yangtze, apparently loading logs onto its deck. I asked the harbor official whether the logs had been floated down the Yangtze as rafts: 'They are pine wood from the United States,' came the reply. 'Oh,' I exclaimed as if I also felt nothing was out of the ordinary. But it was April 3, 1986, ten days after American planes first struck at Tripoli!

Amidst all the different boats, our Zodiac was quite unique. I had originally ordered a gray boat to keep a low profile. But instead, they sent me a bright red one! The commotion we raised as we drove to the lake front of Honghu was phenomenal. Crowds gathered in awe as we inflated the pile of rubber into a 12-foot boat within 30 minutes and sped away.

Our bright red Zodiac attracts a crowd

Honghu is a pristine and unpolluted lake, some 430 square kilometers in area. Ironically, it is situated along the Yangtze between the heavily polluted industrial city of Wuhan and the light industrial city of Shashi. Like many other lakes along the river, it can serve as a regulating valve in flood or drought during different years.

Fishermen with small wooden boats share the lake with tens of thousands of wintering ducks and other waterfowl. Of ducks, there are 18 different kinds. Our intention was to see the duck hunters at work.

The water here was shallow, with continuous vegetation a couple of meters beneath the surface and we had to dodge around a maze of surface nets put there by the fishermen. Little did we know there was another labyrinth of invisible, sub-surface fishing nets.

A fisherman sets out his nets

Forty-three matchlock cannons lined up on three boats

Since the lake never had motorized boats, no markings were needed to lay these nets, except at the ends. Suddenly, little wooden boats raced toward us from all directions. Our outboard had ripped apart seven sets of fishing nets! Furious and cursing at our strange vehicle, the fishermen surrounded it as if they were afraid it might get away. It wasn't until we apologized profusely and explained the purpose of our presence that we were allowed to proceed — this time, at a very cautious speed and guided by a local fisherman.

But, without our guide, it truly would have been a wild goose chase! With him on board, it still took us over two hours to locate the duck hunters. Each group was composed of some 20 wooden boats with two or more people on board. Three of these boats were lined up abreast, on top of which were laid 43 matchlock cannons. Each cannon weighed over 50 kilograms and measured three meters long. After camouflaging the cannons with weeds and straw, the boats were pulled to an open area on the lake with two hunters hiding on board. This patient pair stayed covered for the next few hours.

The remaining boats were then dispatched in all directions to round up the ducks. Over the next few hours, ducks and waterfowl of all description were slowly driven in the direction of the camouflaged boats until they all settled along the vicinity of the cannons. I had long since lost patience and was sleeping on deck when my guide aroused me. The actual hunt was about to begin.

A cloud of white smoke shot up over the horizon followed by a low booming sound. The sky was immediately filled with fowl taking flight. Boats darted toward the center of the burst, a similar sight to the earlier pursuit of our Zodiac, except this time we were among the participants!

Soon, we saw hundreds of birds floating on the lake as we neared the camouflaged boats. Some were still hopelessly trying to take flight. Men with long spears chased these lame ducks without mercy and in no time, front decks were covered with piles of birds.

We paddled to the lead boat where a man tallied deliveries. The initial count totaled 153 birds, mainly mud hens. At this time of year, the ducks had already gone north and only mud hens and 'guardian ducks', thus named as they stay on the lake all year round, remained.

Cigarette in one hand and abacus in the other, Xing Ziguang reassured me that during the height of the season, the men shoot down a couple of thousand birds with one blast — an economically sound, but ecologically dubious, feat. The rest of the hunters were already busy at work retrieving the lost cannons at the bottom of the lake. Drying and resetting them would take half a day, then another round of fruitful harvest, or wholesale slaughter, could take place. In keeping with general protocol, we feasted on mud hens in the evening and spent the night on Xing's master boat.

Guitar music replaced *The East is Red* over our loudspeaker system, as we prepared for another trip upstream. Jeff, who used to be a salmon and crab fisherman from the Puget Sound of Washington, was noticeably disturbed by the previous day's events. We had only been made to pay 100 yuan (US$32) compensation for the seven nets, which he felt was hardly enough. Little did we know we would be grossly overcharged on another fishing event later on, at Yichang further up the Yangtze.

The lame ducks are picked up with long spears

THE MIDDLE REACHES

At Yichang I asked to visit the research institute in charge of the Save the Giant China Sturgeon Project. Due to the construction of China's largest dam at Gezhouba on the Yangtze, this prehistoric fish cannot return to its traditional spawning grounds. With its outward appearance resembling a serpent or dragon, the fish has been likened to these mythical beings by fishermen living along the Yangtze. It grows to nearly half a ton in the ocean before returning to the upper Yangtze to lay its eggs. To do this, it has to swim almost 3,000 kilometers inland to Yibin, 370 kilometers upstream from Chongqing.

Despite the alarm of marine biologists, the dam was built as scheduled. A number of institutes were put in charge of coordinating research to save the giant China sturgeon (*Acipenser sinensis*). Fish ladders were discussed but never got beyond the drawing board. Finally, two other plans were adopted. In the first, mature sturgeons are captured to produce eggs for artificial insemination. In the second, sturgeons are caught in the fall, transported above the dam and released to continue their swim upstream. How and whether these creatures ever return to the ocean we don't know.

At the research institute, we got into the huge fish tank and swam with six giant specimens. Their mild temperaments were deceiving and, as we

The giant China sturgeon in different liquids

The medicine man sells his wares

closed in for photography, Yi Jifeng, a sturgeon expert, warned us not to get too casual with the fish: 'In excitement, be it from happiness or anger, the sturgeon might strike with its tail. I was playing with one the other week and the next thing I knew, I was in bed for three days with an aching back.' My feelings of friendship toward the fish decreased after this story and vanished altogether when we were charged 1,000 yuan for entering the tank!

Chinese preservation policy is fragile and an appeal must also be made for another endangered species along the Yangtze, *Alligator sinensis*, more commonly known as the Yangtze alligator, and a close relative of the Mississippi alligator. It lives only in tributaries between Wuhu and Anqing in Anhui Province, in the lower Yangtze.

The Chinese people have utilized these alligators since antiquity. Alligator hide was used in the making of battle drums as early as the Spring and Autumn Period, 3,000 years ago. These drums were said to have an unmatched quality of sound retention, in fair weather or in rain. But perhaps the Chinese waged too many battles as the Yangtze alligator population has dwindled to about 500 in the wild and is now a Class A protected animal in China.

On my first day in Wuhu, I saw a medicine man selling his wares and services. Against the wall behind him was an assortment of skins and bones, the most prominent being a whole alligator skin, about two meters long. Since the animal is of medicinal value, a full skin was selling at 200 yuan and the head of a small alligator at 20 yuan. This trade was openly conducted at a major intersection in the city, only two hours from Xuan-cheng, the alligator preservation project. I asked whether people questioned the 'doctor' about his alligators. 'The only questions people ever have are about prices,' was his reply.

Nor was the building of Gezhouba Dam controversial in China. Considering the power it would generate, the navigational advantages and its capacity to regulate flooding and irrigation, it simply had to be built. This was especially true during those years when productivity and politics were guiding factors to a developing nation and revolution took precedence over conservation. A tiny jellyfish, once familiar to the kids who lived in the neighborhood of the dam, has not been seen since the dam was completed. One can only hope future dams will not deplete more species.

Like many other projects begun in China during the '60s and '70s, the Gezhouba Dam was given a mysterious name, 330 Project. Construction of the first dam across the Yangtze commenced on 30 December 1970 — the 78th birthday of Mao Tsetung. After ten long years, the workers finally diverted the flow of the Yangtze through a secondary channel and brought the 2,561-meter dam to a close.

Building the Gezhouba dam

In doing so, China created a vast machine over the Yangtze which 'liberates' 14 billion kilowatt-hours of electricity annually through its 21 turbogenerators. 'The largest generator (170 megawatt), if installed along the Yellow River, China's second largest river but with only one-twentieth the Yangtze's flow, could not even move a blade,' our guide at the dam said. He made another emphatic comparison: 'The amount of electricity generated here is over three times the national total of 1949.' Somehow, with the modernization program in full swing, most figures and statistics still take 1949, the year the People's Republic was formed, as a basis of comparison, without taking into account population growth and all other variables. A more graphic comparison, and perhaps one that makes the Chinese look like conservationists, is that this amount of electricity can support the needs of 30 million Chinese. The same amount of electricity, however, would only support 1.2 million Americans!

Three locks link the higher river with the water below the dam. Two are 280 meters long and 34 meters wide — enough to allow passage of a fleet of barges totaling over 10,000 tons. A third, smaller lock can accommodate ships under 3,000 tons. Our small inflatable boat was the first boat from outside of China to go through the locks.

An arrangement was worked out for us to pass the locks early in the morning. Two of the staff from the Gezhouba Administration Office came along, one a pilot and the other a security officer. We left the pier at Yichang and cruised slowly upriver toward the dam. Yang Hanshen, the security officer, maintained constant radio contact with the dam's control tower. Soon we were at the entrance channel at the foot of the dam. Mooring to the bank of the channel, we waited in line with a few other early boats for permission to proceed.

The 12-storey, 600-ton lock gate closes us in

A large ship moves through the lock

I hopped onto a passenger cruiser and chatted with its jolly old captain. Captain Luo was 63 years old and began working on the stretch between Yichang and Chongqing in 1944. 'I started working on a boat at the age of 15 and rose through the ranks. First on the deck, then the kitchen, the engine room, second mate, first mate, and now, captain. It was a long, slow journey, just like riding the boat on the Yangtze in those days,' Luo recounted. 'Today, with 1,200 horses behind me, my boat can make the trip from here to Chongqing and back in six days. And he,' Luo said pointing to his first mate on the bridge, 'is 42 years old and graduated from the Marine Institute at Wuhan. Remember the old Chinese saying: "Changjiang's wave from behind pushing the wave in front." He will replace me as captain later this year and I am going to take a cruise up the gorges without anything to worry about, ha, ha.' Captain Luo, apparently, wasn't afraid of retiring.

As we chatted, the 12-storey, 600-ton gate to the lock opened and a few boats descended the dam. I motioned for our Zodiac to move ahead as I was enjoying Captain Luo's casual quips and optimism, something I wasn't expecting to get from either official on my boat. We steamed ahead slowly as the first mate took to the helm and gave orders below deck. Captain Luo laid back a bit, as if contemplating his cruise after retirement. Our boats looked like David and Goliath, with our small vessel tiny beside Captain Luo's *Dongfanghong* ('The East is Red') *Number 31*. The gate closed behind us and we slowly rose up the walls as water began to fill the lock. It took roughly 15 minutes to fill the lock with 300,000 cubic meters of water.

'How many horses do you have behind you?' Captain Luo turned his interest to our boat. 'Twenty five,' I replied, feeling a little intimidated, 'but I can go 15 to 20 kilometers an hour,' I quickly added. 'We knew you were coming. The Yichang Yangtze Administration notified all the larger ships in

the gorges to reduce to the slowest speed on encountering your "red thing",' the captain replied. I felt a little hurt. 'But you should still be very careful as you go up the three gorges,' Luo said, taking on a more serious tone. 'The Changjiang is really 12 different rivers here, one for each month of the year. The rise and fall of river level create different problems for navigation. During the dry season, some of the channels can only afford single passage from one direction at a time. Going upriver, we have to yield to downriver traffic as they have more difficulty in stopping. For us, the dam has really helped in smoothing out some of the rapids. What used to be called "Devil's Threshold" and "Coffin Gorge" no longer live up to their names.' Captain Luo then invited me to join his younger crew at the nightly disco on board. I politely declined, as I knew we would be sailing at a much slower pace.

Controlling the movement of boats

The red triangle means one-way traffic only

THE GORGES

The famous Three Gorges cut through a series of limestone mountains which, for centuries, shielded the rich and productive basin of Sichuan from the rest of China's dynastic turmoils. In the past, shipwrecks were frequent along this 204-kilometer stretch of the Yangtze. Countless boatmen and passengers died when their ships perished in a series of deadly rapids.

Today, only a few inscriptions and images of deities on the face of the precipitous cliff tell tales of a darker age. As the water rises, these gods attend to the underwater cemeteries of the drowned people. As it recedes, the images and inscriptions gradually surface to bless the people passing by.

Here, I cannot help but remember a description by an earlier traveler up the Yangtze gorges. Colonel Bailey wrote about his river journey in 1911: 'We were accompanied by a red boat. These are official life-saving boats which hang about the rapids to pick up the unfortunate ones. The story goes that originally the boatmen were paid one dollar for every corpse they recovered, but for a live man only what he could afford to give, consequently men were held under by the life-savers until they were worth a dollar for certain!'

Sandouping is 40 kilometers into the gorge. For years, plans were being made for a second and larger dam to be built across the Yangtze at this point. Indeed, the plans and their future implications loom so large that a special commission has been studying the possibility of establishing a new province, Three Gorges Province.

What final form this dam will take is still under heated debate. The primary issue is whether to construct a 195-meter-high dam, thus raising the water level to 180 meters above sea level, or a lower one of 165 meters which will raise the water level to 150 meters. Either choice would mean flooding huge tracts of land and the displacement of over one million residents inside the gorges. The dam will change the environment and eco-

Sawing wood brought from upriver

The village of Meirendao

system irreversibly, and this is a matter of great concern to many scientists inside and outside of China. Many historic cities will be submerged, as will the famed scenery of the Three Gorges.

On the positive side, navigation will be greatly improved all the way to Chongqing, some 600 kilometers upstream. The new dam's colossal machines will generate 13,000 megawatts of electricity. The completion of the dam should also spell an end to the historical flooding along the middle and lower Yangtze. As one official put it, referring to the disaster that killed 30,000 people and inundated 2.8 million hectares of farmland: 'If the 1954 flood were to recur, the resulting economic losses would be enough to build a Three Gorges Dam.'

Since China opened her door to tourism a few years ago, one of the most popular tours is to cruise through the Three Gorges. The three-day trip from Chongqing to Wuhan is heavily booked all year round. As we sailed inside the gorges, we encountered many of these cruise ships. Some were converted 900-passenger boats which now house 30 or more pampered tourists of the Western world, served by a crew of over 200! True to what Captain Luo said, they all seemed to slow down on approaching us; whether out of consideration or just to have a better look at us, I never could tell.

We explored interesting villages along the bank inside the gorge. One such village was Meirendao (Beauty Islet). Three generations of a clan lived there with few outsiders and just about everybody's last name was Han. Li Xianlu was an exception. He was 57 years old and had immigrated from Yichang. Li owned a village store that sold cigarettes, liquor, biscuits, detergent, soap, matches and little else. Realizing a modest profit of less than two yuan a day, he found life peaceful — that is, until he heard of the forced relocation plans.

The government has already ordered at least 240 people and their families to move to higher ground once the new dam is completed. In compensation, each family will be given 500 yuan.

As we talked, Li produced a pomelo stored away since the previous season, opened it and gave me two slices. Juicy and sweet, it was a pricey item at that time of the year. Pomelo and mandarin oranges grow in the region. Mandarin orchards take up 80 percent of land in some villages, I was told.

The Three Gorges is also the historical home of the kiwi fruit. Grown in the wild, it is called *meihoutou* in Chinese, meaning 'monkey fruit'. Perhaps monkeys like them, an early visitor from New Zealand certainly did and now the fruit is generally believed to have come from the South Pacific islands! Realizing the new economic value of the fruit, a factory was built in Badong, a city of 250,000 inside the gorge, to make wine from kiwi and to can the fruit.

At Badong, we visited a radio station. The geography of the gorges restricts television reception, so radio plays a much more prominent role here. Perched on the window sill of my hotel room, I listened to the broadcast of a popular program called 'Clubhouse of the Countryside' featuring local folk songs. I noticed that the windows facing the streets were considered to have the best views; the river view is considered unattractive since all rubbish and sewage are disposed of along the riverside.

At Wanxian, a sizable city at the upper end of the gorge, such drainage of refuse into the Yangtze is in even more visible proportions. I asked to visit a plant which I had seen dumping large quantities of foamy water into the

Badong radio station

The city of Badong

31

Yangtze, drifting downriver visibly for many kilometers, and invisibly for many more. Instead, I was taken to the Environmental Protection Agency (EPA).

'We were first formed in 1977 and we are a relatively young agency,' Sun Ping said apologetically. He had been told beforehand of the intention of my visit. 'Pollution is still a new word for many Chinese and we are trying very hard to educate the public to be aware of the issue.' I asked about the factory with the foamy excretion again. 'Oh, you mean the Wanxian Papermill. You know, that is a very old papermill,' said Sun. I could hear from his voice that he meant a papermill very senior in rank. 'Their drainage is not very pretty, and it has not met the standard set forth by the government,' he finally conceded, 'but then, they continue to pay the fine we levy on them. You know, they have their hardships.' Sun was excusing or defending the factory over which he probably could not enforce his regulations. 'Once the new dam is finished, they have to move and build a new plant, which they have assured us will be up to standard. Right now, they can afford the fines more than they can afford to modernize their cleaning system,' he told me.

Pollution from the papermill

The same attitude was held by Zhang Xunhong, manager of the Shashi Papermill. Zhang told me during my visit that their factory had been paying approximately 10,000 yuan in fines per year for four to five years already and that it turned out to be a better 'bargain' than making structural changes. The remedial machinery was said to cost over one million yuan. Somehow, the EPA is looked at by many factory managers as being regressive for a nation trying hard to modernize.

No story of the gorges can be considered complete without tales about the trackers. In the past, as boats ascended the river gorges against the rapids, men, sometimes as many as 200, were made to tow the boats slowly upriver as they tracked along the banks. Countless people must have died as they slipped off the precipitous paths into the rapids below. Many worked so they could have two meager meals a day. Today, there are only a few trackers as most boats are powered by diesel engines.

Men tow the boats upriver against the current

CHONGQING TO YIBIN

With over six million people, Chongqing is the third-largest city of the most populous nation on earth. Few people who have seen the crowds at Chongqing would question that. The city, which lies at the confluence of the Jialing River with the Yangtze, is built on the hillside. Called one of the three infernos along the Yangtze (the others are Nanjing and Wuhan), its summer temperatures sizzle at 40° C with a humidity twice as high. Long stairs go up the pier and one wonders why streets are not built closer to the waterfront. It is because the water of the Yangtze here can swell by 400 percent and can fluctuate by as much as 40 meters during high and low water.

Chongqing Military Factory manufactures Yamaha motorcycles these days. As a joint venture with the Japanese, a section of this plant has been converted to produce 80-cc Yamaha motorcycles and another domestic version of the 50-cc motorcycle. Though over 200,000 motorcycles were produced in 1984, five times the amount of the previous year, supply still falls far short of the six million motorcycles on order. Signaling China's entry into consumerism, all of these motorcycles are destined for a burgeoning private market, rather than for military or government use, which the factory used to cater to in the past. Most big Chinese cities are crowded with bicycles, but hilly Chongqing is not conducive to biking. Soon, however, the city will be flooded with the locally produced motorcycles.

Wall markings show the flood level of July, 1981

Manufacturing Yamaha motorcycles

Bridge over the Yangtze at Nanjing

A red and white hovercraft speeds downriver

Customary to Chinese belief that nothing should be put to waste, everything along the Yangtze is utilized somehow. The reeds growing wild along the banks are used for paper-making; the colorful rocks here are used in the construction of houses. We went down to the riverbank and visited some seasonal workers digging gravel. Living in makeshift sheds, they come from the countryside to eke out a living along the city's periphery. One young lady I spoke with was sorting out a heap of rocks, separating the rounded and colorful ones from the unsightly ones. 'Every year after the high-water season, new rocks are carried down the Yangtze and once the river recedes, we come here to work,' explained the girl Li Ling. I asked how much digging could be done in a day as the work looked rather strenuous. 'I can clear 2,000 catties (1,200 kilos) per day by working ten to twelve hours and I earn two yuan,' Li answered with an attractive Sichuan accent.

Above these rocky banks is the Yangtze bridge of Chongqing. Only four such bridges span the entire middle and lower Yangtze along its 2,500-kilometer length. Here, I remembered the introduction a guide delivered to a group of American tourists on a visit to the bridge at Nanjing. After giving some history of the inconvenience before the bridge was built, the woman guide proceeded to explain, with the help of a model, the structural design and construction data of the Nanjing Bridge. Much emphasis was placed on the fact that such a complicated bridge was built without any foreign help. One American bluntly said: 'But I don't see what the big deal is.' The guide answered with a disarming smile: 'That's just like we don't see why Americans collect things a hundred years old and call them antiques!'

We left Chongqing and headed upstream, our moods changing with the mood of the river. We were embarking on a stretch of water little known to foreigners. Many permit applications had been made, but the Chinese government had not granted any for outsiders to sail beyond Chongqing, let alone for anyone to travel in their own boat. From here on, we sailed into the unknown. For long stretches, the road did not intersect with the river, and the Landcruiser could only serve as support at infrequent intervals. We camped out constantly, and gasoline for the boat became our major concern.

The message that we were in an unexplored territory came fast. On our first morning sailing above Chongqing as we cruised close to the bank, our outboard grounded, and the propeller was wrecked. We pulled the boat onto a sandy beach and Jeff installed one of our three spare propellers. It was here that we saw a red and white hovercraft speeding downriver — a very unexpected sight. It was one of three experimental hovercrafts China had built to serve the river between Yibin and Chongqing.

During the first afternoon, we encountered huge bamboo rafts going downriver. Harvested bamboo from southern Sichuan and northern Guizhou provinces was bound together into structures larger than tennis courts, and floated downriver to Chongqing and Wanxian. We tied our boat alongside

A team of men work a huge bamboo raft

one and boarded the seemingly rickety raft for a short chat with the crew. To my surprise, it was more stable than our boat.

A team of five men worked the raft, two in front, two in the back and one, apparently the captain, stayed amidships next to a shed to give orders. There was no real stern or bow. Each end had one extra-long oar which also acted as the helm. And as the raft turned in half circles when it negotiated river bends, what was formerly the bow would suddenly become the stern.

Liu Huaqian, the person amidships, had floated rafts for 12 years. 'This *pai* (rafts tied into barges) is 2,500 catties in weight and it takes nine days to make the trip from Hejiang to Changshou, a distance of roughly 300 kilometers,' he explained. 'Isn't it pretty hard work putting the raft together?' I asked. 'With their help', Liu answered pointing to his crew, 'I can have it done in three days.'

That evening, just before stopping to camp for the first time along the banks of the Yangtze, we wrecked and replaced another propeller. But we had one consolation — the door of our tent faced a majestic monastery on the opposite bank.

After our freeze-dried stroganoff, a nice change from the hot spicy Sichuan diet we'd been having for the last two weeks, we made a run across the river to visit the monastery. The multi-storey temple had been abandoned since the Cultural Revolution. It was called Big Buddha Monastery and one old man was taking care of the premises at the time of our visit.

We broke camp early in the morning to continue our trip upriver. Except for a few small fishing sampans in the distance, nothing passed us by. All of a sudden, Jeff cut our motor as he shaded his hand above his eyes to look back east, toward a group of fishing boats that we had just passed.

'I swear something just hopped out of the river onto one of those boats,' Jeff said to me as he turned the head of our Zodiac around. 'Oh yeah? Did we cut across their bow that close?' I asked jokingly, in reference to the ghosts that would be left behind. But Jeff was in no mood for jokes. His fisherman instinct told him something was fishy.

Within a few minutes we were closing in on this group of four sampans. Jeff was right. A tiny animal rested on the bow of each of these boats. We could hardly believe our eyes when these animals turned out to be river otters.

A river otter catches fish for its owner

'We use river otters to fish in the Yangtze,' the sampan-owner told me. This discovery was so exciting that I forgot to ask for permission before boarding their sampan and almost tipped it over with my weight. But soon I had settled down, close against the owner near the canopied center of the sampan.

Jeff moored the Zodiac next to the sampan. As I talked with the fisherman, he kept asking me to translate what had been said. I had never seen him so attentive!

'They are not caught locally but purchased from Tibet. An otter skin would cost you only 300 yuan, but for a live one, we pay 2,000 yuan,' said 59-year-old Li Xiaoqing. 'But they are excellent fishermen, better even than cormorants. On an average day, he can get me 20 to 30 catties of fish.' Given such a big investment, the otter would need to be productive. Li asserted that his investment was recouped within five months of active fishing. 'It takes two to three months just to train an otter and I have to feed it two catties of fish a day', Li spoke as he playfully lured an otter with a small fish to make it stand on two feet. My eyes were drawn to Li's fingers, which had many scars. Training the otters had apparently taken its toll, but his fingers had survived five otters in 38 years. 'Very few people know how to train otters these days. I was taught by my parents. What you see here is just about all that's left. Maybe four more families upstream own otters. But that is it,' said Li with pride in his face.

I asked to observe them at work, but it was not to be. The otters only fish at night; they had just finished their outing and were on their way to a nearby market as we caught up with them. We made an appointment to meet them at one of their favorite spots that evening. As we talked, the otter jumped off the boat, swam alongside for a moment, then climbed on board again. All the while, it was attached to the boat by a rope around its body. We proceeded to Hejiang looking forward to an evening with the otters.

Hejiang lies at the confluence of the Yangtze River with the Chishui River (Red River) coming down from Guizhou and is famous for its lychee fruit. It was said that during the Tang Dynasty, Emperor Ming Huang ordered that this juicy fruit be carried by a relay of horsemen all the way to Chang'an (today's Xian) in exchange for a smile from his favorite concubine, Yang Guifei. But we came too late to verify the story and too early to have a taste of the lovely fruit!

However, at a teahouse down the main street, we tried something else with a local flavor. Over tea and conversation, crowds gathered to view the weekly bird fight popular among residents of Hejiang. Birdcages covered with blinds lined one side of the teahouse. On a raised platform in the center was a specially made cage with a central partition. As the crowd cheered, a bald man, the referee and announcer, came up front to take his position behind the cage. He announced the names of two men whose birds would be on stage next. Behind him in the courtyard, two older men were busily preparing their *huameis*, Painted Brow, as these fighting birds are called because of two white rings around their eyes.

A female huamei in a cage was put up close to the two males readying themselves for the fight. In contest for her patronage, both males started whistling away at the lady, who seemed bemused and kept wiggling her tail. At the height of their excitement, the female was taken away and the two males were put on stage at each end of the special center cage.

As the doors to their respective cages were lifted, the two aroused huameis rushed to the center and fought each other with their claws and beaks. Every now and then, they withdrew to the far ends of the cage, waited, screeched, then re-entered the ring and fought for another round. The bald man meanwhile, with the urgency of an auctioneer, described the close-up scene of the battle. His listeners forgot about their tea and waited anxiously for the final verdict.

The first two birds were beautifully matched for half a dozen rounds and were considered tied. Many other battles were settled within a couple of rounds, when one of the birds would retreat into his own cage. Still others ended with a clear loser that did not dare to advance to the center partition at all, to the booing of a disappointed crowd!

Fighting huameis *at a Hejiang teahouse*

Jeff inspects the wrecked propeller

Buses run on the natural gas carried on their roofs

That evening, we sailed upstream to our rendezvous with the otter fisherman. Our local guide assured us he knew the river well enough for us to sail at night. We hit bottom twice; the second time the entire boat came to a halt on shore before we knew what was happening. We limped back to town to fetch our one remaining propeller from the Landcruiser. Since we had already made other plans for the next morning, our intention to document the otters had to be postponed to another night.

The next morning we motored up Chishui River. We'd been told that boatmen here can balance themselves on one huge bamboo pole by using a second bamboo pole as an oar. Less than ten kilometers into this tributary, however, our exploration was again cut short by the same guide who had grounded us the previous night. The only difference was that this time we hit ground so hard that the entire cover of our outboard flew away and our last propeller shattered. Jeff was all profanity and suspected a conspiracy was going on to end our excursion in a disgraceful manner. I was in no mood to save the wretched guide from Jeff's verbal assault. 'With pilots like this, I can understand why the Chinese are developing hovercrafts,' Jeff said sarcastically.

We left Hejiang in despair, knowing it would require a return trip to study the river otters and the boatmen on single bamboo. Worse still, now we would have to abandon our boat until a fresh supply of propellers and, more important still, a depth finder, could be flown in.

We continued on with our jeep, staying as close to the river as possible. Luzhou was only a couple of hours drive west of Hejiang. There we encountered public buses with gigantic balloons on their roofs, which turned out to be rubber tanks holding natural gas. Just about all the buses of Luzhou were gas operated. It is cheaper and cleaner, but each 'tankful' lasts only 50 kilometers.

Luzhou is a major natural-gas-producing area of China and its residents lead the rest of the nation in burning gas in homes. The first gas well was drilled along the Yangtze in 1956. Today, that same well is still in service, having produced over 600 million cubic meters of gas. Given that each well costs two million yuan to drill, and each 100 million cubic meters can earn 20 million yuan, Well Number One is a clear winner for the government-owned gas company.

Yibin is 123 kilometers upriver from Luzhou. A famous wine city, the aromatic scent of liquor filled the air as we drove by some of the distilleries. Today, Yibin is one of the oldest distillation capitals in the world, boasting a history of over 1,200 years of liquor-making and one 500-year-old cellar which is still in service. A local saying goes: 'One man drinks and a thousand are intoxicated, one bottle opens and the entire city fills with fragrance.'

One of the most sought-after liquors in the Chinese market is Wuliangye (Five Grains Extract). We visited their plant and observed the traditional process of distillation. In 1984, 30 tons of this high-proof liquor were produced; demand has driven the price per bottle from under ten yuan to over 30 on the black market. We spent our last hour at the plant, tasting the 'Extract' in all of its varieties, and left happy and somewhat light-headed.

Next stop was the Hanging Coffins south of Yibin. Suspended from precipitous cliffs along some tributaries of the Yangtze near Gongxian, the coffins of the Bo people remain a mystery to this day. Perhaps to deter grave looters, perhaps inspired by a religious belief, the Bo must have been strongly determined to put these coffins in the most inaccessible places. While the coffins of their ancestors remain, the Bo, once a large ethnic minority roaming southern China, suddenly disappeared some three centuries ago. Primitive wall paintings with pictographs of people, animals, geometric designs and other symbols adorn these cliffs and add to the, already haunting, effect. Undaunted by such predecessors, today some Miao and Han people make these hills and valleys their homes.

Bottling a popular local liquor

THE JINSHAJIANG

From Yibin we took a local passenger boat, *Red Guard Number One*, for the ten-hour run up the Jinshajiang (River of Golden Sand), past Pingshan, to Xinshizhen. From Yibin, the Yangtze adopts this new name for the next 2,300 kilometers. The name changed again as we reached Qinghai Province where it became Tongtianhe (River to Heaven) or Dri Qu (Female Yak River) for the Tibetans. It is also called Tuotuohe (Red River in Mongol) near the glacier source, and Dam Qu (Marsh River) near the marshland source. The great river has so many different names as it flows through many different ethnic areas and each local group has its own traditional name for it.

Hanging Coffins

A sampan on the Jinshajiang

As the boat ascended the river, it was climbing against a fast yellowish current and lifting up 38 meters over the next 62 kilometers to Pingshan. In certain areas, the river dropped for half to one meter, thus creating rapids which sometimes broadsided the boat. The boat made two routine stops. Each time, the captain simply ploughed the boat onto the sandy bank; a gangplank was pulled off the bow which connected the tip of the boat to the shore as people went on and off.

When Xinshizhen was in sight, a sailor took some pigeons out on deck and released them into the bright blue sky. I asked where the pigeons were heading. 'This stretch of water is so treacherous that we have to let Yibin know we have arrived safely,' said the man.

Releasing the pigeons

Raising pigeons has become such a popular sport that in Nanjing the Sports Federation has formed a society for its enthusiasts, which has over 10,000 members in Nanjing alone. A pigeon called Yudian (Raindrop), did an incredible 2,310-kilometer return flight from Liuyuan along the Silk Road and back to Nanjing. I said that next time I'd take Yudian along to break the record as we were now over 3,000 kilometers upriver from Nanjing.

Xinshizhen is the upper end for boat traffic on the Yangtze. Beyond, the river becomes a torrent with rapids and sudden drops that make navigation impossible. As I looked upriver, I could see the Yangtze disappearing into a series of narrow gorges. We had left the agricultural plains of the middle Yangtze and the fertile basin of Sichuan for good; from here on, the river cut through mountain ranges. The only farming to be seen was on terraces along the hillside. We could only travel in our Landcruiser from here, cutting across the Yangtze and exploring on foot wherever we could.

Xinshizhen is also the demarcation line between the Han people and the Yi ethnic minority group. A footpath along the Yangtze leads up to Leibo, an autonomous county of the Yi people. Leibo, meaning in Chinese 'Thunder and Wave', lived up to its name. We saw black clouds gathered above the ravaging Yangtze as a thunderstorm developed.

But the rain did not stop us from visiting Yi villages. In one, a lady performed a musical tune for us with her *kouqin* (mouth organ), shaped like a jew's harp. The sound was soft as a whisper and no doubt invented for courtship as one had to sit intimately close to the performer in order to hear anything. We finished our visit by joining a funeral party, where Yi relatives and friends of a deceased girl drank to their hearts' content.

In nearby Butuo County, a Sunday market was taking place. I was impressed with the Yi's fine woodwork. The market was full of colorfully dressed Yi women from the countryside. I purchased some wooden bowls, cups and a horse saddle with traditional designs in red, yellow and black painted on them. As I was putting my purchases away, I saw a huge crowd marching down the street. In the front was a Yi man wearing a black turban and walking with a black sheep held on a leash.

An Yi man draws his sheep forward

My instinct wrongly told me that they must be taking the animal to some ritual sacrifice. Hurriedly, I followed the crowd. As we marched through the center of town, more people joined us. Within a short while, we were on the other side of town and everyone halted at a field where more people had already gathered. As it turned out, the black sheep I followed, and half a dozen more, were heroes of the day, rather than victims.

The crowd formed a ring, with men and children in front and women mainly at the back of the crowd. Two sheep were brought into the ring. A sheep was held by a man at each side of the circle. These creatures looked stronger than domestic sheep, more like the bighorn sheep of North America. The two eyed each other intently. As the noise level of the crowd rose, the sheep were released. Immediately, a trail of dust was raised as

Yi women

Two sheep charge each other

41

An Yi child wears a brilliantly embroidered cap

Northwestern Yunnan

they charged at each other at full speed and with lowered heads. A solid thud was heard as the rams met. Then each sheep backed up slowly until they were about 20 meters apart, they then eyed each other for a while, and charged again.

As the crowd cheered them on, the ring became smaller, with spectators pushing in from the outer circle. Yi men with wooden sticks began beating at children and adults alike, trying, in vain, to push the crowd backward to make room for the sheep. As the crowd got more excited, the game was interrupted, I knew that it was time for us to move on!

It was the end of April when we reached Qiaojia, in northeastern Yunnan. We explored the area and saw many dramatic white-water rapids within the 20-kilometer stretch north of Qiaojia. At dusk, we bade farewell to the River of Golden Sand, which had appropriately taken on the color of the setting sun. This was the last town along the Yangtze we were to visit before returning to the US for a brief break to reassess our plans and refurbish our supplies.

THE UPPER REACHES

The beginning of June found us again in China, continuing our travels up the Yangtze. From now on, we would be aiming for the upper reaches and the source of the river. A second Landcruiser was added. We knew that somewhere up in the high plateau we'd need one vehicle to pull the other one out of trouble. An off-road motorcycle was to be used for short-distance explorations and reconnaissance.

My drivers from Canton, Bumpy and Shorty, drove the two jeeps to Kunming. Warren, Jeff and I flew there from Canton. The main constraints for this stretch of the journey were supply versus space and weather. For example, the food had to be evenly rationed over the next four-month period, the seasonal limit of operating on the plateau.

We left Kunming and proceeded west toward the Yangtze, traveling along the old Burma Road which was built under the direction of General Stilwell during the Second World War. This road, which served as a major support line for supplies to China during the war years, winds through the mountainous regions of southern China. We arrived in Dali, 400 kilometers away, after a day.

Though most of China's mountain ranges go in a west–east direction, the Hengduan Range cuts across the high plateau of eastern Tibet all the way to Yunnan by a north–south route. Thus river systems in that region change their courses and flow south accordingly. These include the Nu (Salween), the Lancang (Mekong) and the Yangtze. As these rivers enter northwestern Yunnan, they cut through granite and alluvium mountains and leave in their trails some of the most spectacular gorges in the world.

These three great rivers of Asia run almost a parallel course for hundreds of kilometers. At some points in northwestern Yunnan, they come within 50 kilometers of each other, only separated by two narrow watersheds. The Nu and the Lancang continue their southward flow and drain into the sea through Burma and Vietnam respectively. The Yangtze makes a hairpin turn at the town of Shigu, flows north through one of the world's deepest canyons and finally takes an easterly course to the China Sea.

As we approached this spectacularly deep gorge from the south, the river flowed by quietly. Then, as the river dropped into the gorge, it became more of a ravaging torrent than I had seen at any other stretch of the Yangtze. It is called Tiger Leaping Gorge as the river narrows to less than 30 meters and legend has it that a tiger was once seen leaping across it.

Only three Westerners had ever seen Tiger Leaping Gorge, and all of them did so over 50 years ago. It was our intention to explore the full length of this gorge and beyond. At Qiaotou (Bridge Head), preparations were made for us to hike in.

While waiting for me to negotiate for some mules, Warren, a professional pharmacist, acting as this new expedition's medical officer, cried out to Jeff: 'Come on over and look at this!' He was looking down the bank of Hutiaojiang, a tributary which flows into the Yangtze. Jeff went over and I followed.

Warren was smiling broadly as he pointed to a bush along the bank. 'Is that really what I think it is?' asked Warren. 'What do you think?' Jeff said, turning to me. We all knew we were looking at a huge plot of marijuana some six feet high. The security office, the equivalent of a police station, stood within five meters of the plot. Chinese grow hemp and use it for making clothes or ropes. That the plant has another more sedative usage is apparently not known to them!

Warren inspects the local flora

Many mule trains go as far as a tungsten mine halfway into the gorge, 4,000 meters high. We finally convinced a Naxi man to abandon his farm work and guide us into the gorge with his single work-horse carrying our load. Shorty and Bumpy bade us farewell and began driving to Daju, a tiny village at the other end of the gorge, where they would wait for us.

Our trail followed the left bank of the river as we entered the gorge from the south. Workers had recently moved here from Dali and were busily quarrying marble exposed on the cliff face. The quality of the rock was said to surpass even that of the famous Dali marble.

Our guide, Tang Jianwen, was 36 years old. As he led the way, he complained to me about his grim prospects. A few years ago, he was a mechanic at a local brigade under the commune system. As the communes were decentralized and people returned to family-based farming, he found his skills were not needed any more; most people attended to their own handtractors and other simple machines. 'As I was not a farmer before, I wasn't allotted the land which other farmers got,' Tang complained. 'I have raised this issue with the local government many times, but no one seems to be able to do anything.' Tang ended up helping his relatives by working on their plots of land.

Following a hazardous path

The narrow footpath continued. Once in a while we encountered mule trains carrying tungsten mined out of the mountains. When we passed them, we always stayed to the inside of the path and let the caravan take the precipitous cliff side. Over 100 meters below us the Yangtze was a white torrent, cascading through a series of rapids. The sound of gushing water sometimes seemed to echo off the wall of the mountains.

Over a distance of 17 kilometers inside the gorge, the Yangtze drops a dramatic 210 meters. The river is flanked by the Yulong Snow Range, peaking at 5,596 meters, and Harba Snow Mountain at a slightly lower altitude. Both rise over 3,000 meters above the river. The canyon thus formed is, without a doubt, one of the deepest in the world.

That night we camped out along a ledge overlooking the narrowest stretch of the river to the music of the thunderous torrent below and a thunderous storm above. Tang, meanwhile, went ahead to Hetaoyuan (Walnut Garden), a village a couple of kilometers away, to stay with friends. We got our three meals that day, but they all came at one time. We were so hungry that Jeff made 12 portions of freeze-dried food for the four of us!

Camping on a ledge

Local people gather round curiously

The following morning the sky cleared and Tang was back to guide us on. The previous night's rain had washed much of the loose rock off the mountain sides. Here and there were minor mud and rock slides. We moved ourselves forward cautiously until the gorge became slightly wider. At Hetaoyuan, we visited a few families of the Lisu minority who eked out a precarious existence by terracing small plots of land along the hill. They cultivated corn, planted figs and grew barley but, for some strange reason, no walnuts! The men hunted for hares and other small game during their spare time, using homemade crossbows.

We hiked on and by noon arrived at a ledge where a rock slide had effectively covered up the trail. Tang tested the rocks and edged ahead cautiously. Then he backed off and told us to clear a tiny path. When we felt we had done our best, we attempted to usher the horse across.

No matter what we tried, Caoliu ('drifting on grass') would not advance. We pushed, we lured and we begged, but he simply would not budge. Finally, we gave up and decided that perhaps Caoliu knew it was unsafe for him to cross. A decision was made to tether him and for Tang to retrieve him on his way back. One by one, on our hands and knees, we got across the ledge. From there on, the path began to get wider and smoother, but we were hiking at a much slower pace. Had we known all that was packed on Caoliu's back would end up on our own backs, we would not have brought so much.

Gradually Tiger Leaping Gorge widened into a valley. We met a family living in a huge cave with scores of sheep and cattle. They were totally startled by our sudden and odd appearance; no one from outside had come that way for a long time. Tang, by now, was very anxious to go back and fetch Caoliu.

Caoliu would not budge

On the other side of the river was Daju, a remote village on a tableland where a marginal road ended and where Shorty and Bumpy were supposed to be waiting. We tried to negotiate with the family to guide us down to the river to a ferry crossing. But even the substantial sum we offered for them to take us that short distance wouldn't budge them. They were scared of us.

We moved on a bit further until we ran into a mother and child herding animals on the hillside. Tang was becoming more eager by the minute to go back, and negotiated aggressively for a new guide. He even offered to cut his pay from our promised 60 yuan to 50 yuan. Our next guide turned out to be the six-year-old child of the family. As we began hiking upward, his mother yelled at him to come back. He explained that they needed two people to attend to the animals, one for the sheep and the other for the cattle. But I prompted him to continue. So for three yuan he led us to his village where, supposedly, his uncle could show us down the bank to the ferry.

The tiny village had perhaps a dozen houses, but no uncle. The child left us. We found one tall sullen-faced man in a shed, brewing some tea. As we sat down to quench our thirst, we found out it wasn't even his house we had entered. Something was strange here. We saw no other villagers. The man said he supervised a group of criminals confined to hard labor who were building a road up from the river to a logging camp. I was in no mood to check out his story. Another eerie hour passed till he rose, shouldered two of our packs on his back, and led us down to the Yangtze on a hazardous and steep path. Not a word was exchanged along the way.

At the ferry crossing, we felt relieved that a boat was on the other bank. We yelled and waved, but the people there simply took no notice. The river was still gushing fast out of the gorge, which was almost 200 meters wide here. After an hour or so, we finally saw the ferry coming across. Four men on their feet, with their entire bodies bent forward then backward, were

Bumpy had set up the tent inside the room

furiously rowing the wooden boat, which was about ten meters long. As they rowed upriver, the boat was actually going downriver. But their vigorous attempt was slowly propelling the boat toward the center of the river.

I felt some trepidation, knowing that we would soon be on that same ferry. As we watched them battle the waves in the middle current, their cries in low unison were heard over the constant slur of the river. In a few more minutes, they were closing in on our side of the bank, but had drifted further downriver. Soon, to our great surprise, we saw them rowing upriver by the bank with ease. The fast center current had created a reverse flow along the bank. Two men jumped off the boat onto the bank and tracked it upriver with guide lines.

The return trip followed the same routine but with four tense passengers on board. On the other side, I wiped the sweat off my forehead and thanked the oarsmen, paying them our fares of one yuan per head. At low water, the same passage would cost only 0.30 yuan.

Bumpy and Shorty had come down the bank to greet us. We passed our loads to them and proceeded to hike the 200 meters up the other bank to the tableland of Daju. But the village was still a couple of kilometers away. We went to a two-storey building where our jeeps were parked. This was literally the end of the road. As if to remind us of the remote place we were in, the man in charge of the house told us there was a leper colony nearby and this building was its medical headquarters.

I was given the head doctor's office upstairs to sleep in, while Shorty and Bumpy took the adjacent room. On my desk was a thick report about leprosy in China with demographics regarding its distribution. I read it with interest since this kind of material rarely crossed my path. But that evening I found something even more interesting next door. Horrified by the word 'leprosy', Bumpy had set up a tent on the floor inside their room!

About ten kilometers north, or downriver, of Daju is Baidi (White Land). Here we camped in a canyon where the hill was terraced by the Naxi farmers. Further up the hill were terraces of a different nature. Water from two underground springs deposited so many minerals there that an extensive area of white-terraced lakes had been created. This phenomenon intrigued the Naxi so much that they gathered here every year to pray to their gods. Some of these rock formations had taken on mystifying shapes. Different names or objects were affixed to them by the Naxi people. One rock resembled the abdomen of a pregnant lady, thus all women came to pray to this goddess of fertility. The incense and burning of sacred papers had given the pregnant goddess a tan!

One might think that these shapes would change with the continuing deposition of minerals. Not so. The Naxi farmers had diverted the water flow to irrigate their man-made terraces and effectively ended the growth of these natural formations.

We pitched our tents on the lakes. That night we saw fireflies, but none of the flying squirrels which were said to roam the area. We left Baidi and went on to Lijiang, government seat of the Naxi Autonomous Prefecture. The Naxi are a minority nationality of China with approximately a quarter of a million people and a romantic past, recorded in an ancient pictographic script. Those Naxis living on the Lijiang Plain grow wheat, corn and barley. Amongst other unusual characteristics, many Naxis in town keep parrots as house pets and, in the past, Naxi lovers made suicidal pacts and jumped off cliffs of the Yulong Mountain, by the Yangtze.

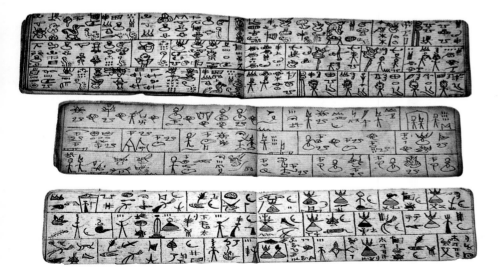

Naxi pictographs

The hotel in town could be considered luxurious or primitive, depending on which direction the traveler had come from. For us, it was comfortable. The latrine facilities were in another building. I always avoided using indoor latrines in remote areas, given so much open space. Jeff and Warren always lit cigarettes before entering one of these places.

We traveled east of Lijiang and reached Sudi, a small village by the Yangtze. Here the river makes an ethnic demarcation; to the west, live the Naxi and to the east, the Lisu, a tribe of northwestern Yunnan. Copper was being mined along the hills here. As we descended toward the river and passed by some miners' houses, we saw signs warning the inhabitants not to leave the vicinity. Obviously these miners were prisoners confined here for hard labor.

Further east, hidden among the hills, the plain of Yongling forms the dividing line between Sichuan and Yunnan provinces. Here, lives a sub-group of the Naxi, the Moso, who maintain a matrilineal family structure. Chinese anthropologists call the Moso a 'living fossil of human society'. Not only is the woman's power and authority absolute at home, she also reigns over every aspect of daily activity from planning and decision-making, to food production and distribution.

Moso matriarch, a 'living fossil'

It is not unusual for a Moso woman to maintain an intimate relationship with a number of *azhus* (lovers) at one time, or scores of azhus over a lifetime. A man visits a woman only nocturnally and returns to his daytime domicile as a productive member of his maternal home. Thus there are no economic ties between the couple. Offspring are products of, in many cases, casual and ephemeral courtship. These people seldom marry, and words like husband and wife, or even father, are relatively new to their vocabulary. Family names usually follow that of the mother's side. Inheritance, likewise, is handed down from mother to daughter, within the family. While customs have been changing with the Moso making a transition into a patrilineal family, a survey done in October 1983 covering 1,878 mature women revealed that 393 still maintain *azhu* relationships.

Reflecting the age-old custom of the Moso, the Lion Rock which dominates the region has long been revered as a sacred goddess. Other peaks in the area are lower and male in gender, as if subservient to the dominating female.

As our jeeps negotiated the curves out of the Moso's mountain enclave, I was still pondering over the philosophy of a matriarch I spoke to: 'Other people look at our form of relationship and wonder why. We look at incessant family feuds and the suffering of the women among our neighboring peoples and wonder why not!'

The roads were constantly getting worse. Instead of being plagued by broken propellers, we were now faced with punctured tires almost everyday. Soon, we had to put tubes into all our tubeless tires. Shorty had never thought much of our imported 'All Terrain' tires that came with glue on the inside for self-patching in the event of a puncture. On another occasion, he laughed at our US$150 advanced hand pump which we worked with great effort to filter water for drinking. He thought a foot pump would save us some strength. He was probably right.

As we traveled north by road toward the high Tibetan Plateau, the river flowed through nomad territories. Following Shorty's first mountain-sickness attack at a logging camp 3,850 meters high, Warren started taking more seriously a local prescription given to me by a Tibetan, the gall of a mountain goat; taken a quarter gall at a time and once every seven days, it was meant to alleviate mountain sickness.

We proceeded through the last towns of Yunnan, passing through Zhongdian, Deqen, Yanjing and finally, into Markam in eastern Tibet. Batang is 70 kilometers beyond Markam, one of the few cultural centers of the plateau.

Lying near the Yangtze, and relatively low in altitude, Batang has a fairly mild climate. It boasts some of the most fertile land in the region and is thus conducive to a settled population. As a result, many cultural forms flourished, among them Batang music, dance and theater.

Upstream 300 kilometers is another important political and cultural center, Dege. The 'king' of Dege traditionally controlled a huge area equivalent to the five present-day counties, all of which lie east and west of the Yangtze. But Dege's claim to fame is perhaps more due to the Dege Treasure House.

My first visit to Dege was in 1982, soon after the Treasure House resumed printing the *Ganjhur*, sacred scriptures of Buddhism. Saved from the devastations of both the 1959 uprising and the ten-year Cultural Revolution, Dege still holds over 217,000 printing blocks which cover disciplines as diverse as religion, history, art, literature, medicine, astronomy and mathematics.

In the past, only 25 copies of the *Ganjhur* were printed every year. Today, with the resurgence of religion and in order to fulfil the great demand, about 200 copies a year must be printed. Anweng, the manager

Tibetan from Markam

Settlement at Batang

The famous monastic printing press

now in charge, said: 'During the Cultural Revolution we did not print a single book. Since printing resumed in 1979, we've been working overtime to make up for lost time.' With such dedication, I have little doubt that Dege Treasure House is the most meritorious production line along the entire Yangtze.

Beyond Dege, the Yangtze soon enters Qinghai Province, a plateau region in excess of 4,000 meters. The headwaters of the Yangtze are here and to reach them, we had to cross eastern Tibet before heading north into Qinghai. This is no easy task given that few roads have been built on the plateau.

Heading west toward Lhasa, our plans quickly altered due to the closing of the Chengdu–Lhasa road. A glacier had shifted so fast during the spring of 1985 that avalanches had destroyed a good section of the road. The only other alternative was to advance through an even more marginal road in northeastern Tibet, beginning in Qamdo, heading north and cutting past Riwoqe, Dengqen, Barqen and Xagquka, a series of high country towns unknown to the rest of the world.

After struggling for ten days, often digging and pulling out one jeep after the other through knee-deep mud, we finally arrived in Lhasa. The few other vehicles we saw along the way were all driven by 'desperados' like ourselves, heading in or out of the high city of Tibet. Unfortunately, no one else had power winches, as we did, and most vehicles ended up hopelessly stranded, some simply abandoned. I passed on my share of mountain sickness to the drivers by constantly attending to my notes and cameras thus leaving them with the bulk of the digging.

THE SOURCE

In Lhasa, we had our last inventory check, readying ourselves for the highlight of our expedition — the exploration of the source of the Yangtze. I found that we were disproportionately low on our supply of Swiss chocolate. It turned out that what was an occasional treat in my lead vehicle had been a staple diet in the second jeep!

For centuries, the source of the Yangtze had baffled Chinese scholars and geographers. Chinese history before the Ming Dynasty (1268–1644) recorded that the 'Great River' originated in northern Sichuan where the Min River, a large tributary of the Yangtze, began its flow. Then came the famous geographer in the mid-16th century, Xu Xiake, who learned through explorations that the Jinsha should be considered the upper reaches of the Yangtze. Later geographers took Xu's work further and pinpointed a mountain of eastern Qinghai as the source of the river. The myth went on and it wasn't until 1976 that the Chinese government organized a major scientific expedition to define the source of the Yangtze.

With a huge retinue of military and logistic support in the air and on the ground, a team of Chinese scientists traveling westward left the road linking Golmud, in central Qinghai, with Lhasa, in Tibet. After struggling with roadless terrain, their caravan of trucks and jeeps arrived at the glacier source of Tuotuohe, one of the main headwaters of the Yangtze. As a result of this expedition, the world was told that the Yangtze originated from Jianggendiru Glacier in Geladandong Peak, the highest peak of the Tanggula Range. Two other important headwaters of the Yangtze in Qinghai Province, Dam Qu and Qumar, were also partially explored. In 1978, another team of Chinese again re-entered the headwaters area and did further research.

Our Landcruisers take us ever closer to the source

Our intentions all along were to explore and document in pictures the geography of the glacier source, then, based on work the Chinese teams had done, explore the source of Dam Qu. Aided by information collected by the two other teams, we hoped to advance the work accomplished by the Chinese in 1976 and 1978. We traveled north from Lhasa, and within two days arrived at Tuotuoheyan, a small town in southern Qinghai along the Golmud–Lhasa Highway. Here the river flowed down from the glacier source at 5,500 meters to 4,800 meters and was about 250 meters wide. A team of government cadres was on hand to greet us. They were sent here to arrange for guides and interpreters, as well as to manage our other logistic needs.

I was told of Yao Maoshu, a student of Jiaotong University at Chengdu. With the help of a Tibetan guide and a yak, he brought a rubber raft to the vicinity of the glacier source in mid-June. Slightly downriver, where the water was deeper, he launched his raft and floated down Tuotuohe. Within three days, he arrived here at the town of Tuotuoheyan and continued downriver. His goal was to raft down the upper Yangtze all the way to Yibin in Sichuan, a feat never before attempted. I was disappointed that I had missed him by a month.

The next morning was July 27. As I walked out of our hostel, the ground was covered with a fresh, but thin, layer of snow. 'Summer' on the high plateau could be deceiving. Deputy Governor Ying of Golmud brought a Tibetan to see me; Dawagonbu became my interpreter for the next two weeks. At 32, Dawa (as I called him) came from Ali in western Tibet and had worked in this area with other Chinese geologists. His brown-corduroy jacket and small cap revealed little of his nomadic past. We drove south for 90 kilometers to Yanshiping, a small town where I picked up my first guide. Guodor was the party secretary of the town, and he accompanied us for two days until a more experienced guide was found.

At Yanshiping, we filled up both jeeps with gasoline. Together with six jerry cans and four rubber tanks that were originally intended for the boat, we had 500 liters, enough to give each Landcruiser 1,000 kilometers on good roads, and 500 kilometers on rough ones. As we had calculated the round trip to the glacier source to be approximately 350 kilometers, we were carrying enough gas to make some side trips.

On July 28, we proceeded to Road Maintenance Station Number 100, 21 kilometers south of Yanshiping. Here we left the road. We drove over a few small creeks, followed an old riverbed, and passed through a valley between some undulating hills. At 4,800 meters, vegetation was sparse and the grass scanty. A few nomadic tents and some small herds of yak and sheep made up the rest of the scenery.

Six kilometers off the main road it started hailing. This hail, and at times snow, hit us over and over again while we were above 5,000 meters. Usually the sky would clear up and the sun would be shining within the next half hour. For the first ten kilometers, the ride was bumpy, but uneventful, as we

Gassing up for the last stretch

followed some old tracks of a marginal road toward an abandoned quartz mine.

The next 35 kilometers took us almost eight hours, most of that time spent in digging, pushing and pulling the jeeps out of the mud. With the exception of the two Tibetans, each of us could only dig a few shovelfuls before stopping to catch our breath. Exhausted from the rarefied air, Shorty commented that the lungs of the Tibetans were well broken in, while ours were broken. I consoled everybody by saying that the Chinese team in 1976 covered only seven kilometers on their first day.

We began seeing small herds of wild yellow goats and rare Tibetan antelopes. We also saw the occasional wild ass. Tall, and sporting a bright-yellow skin, they usually appeared in pairs. In between more digging and towing, Guodor shot an antelope and tied the animal behind our vehicle.

The towering peak of Geladandong was rising in front of us. We came across a group of tents where about 40 Tibetan nomads, all men, were gathering for their horse race. Guodor told me that these Tibetans were members of Jiri village. By village, he meant 20 to 30 widely scattered nomadic tents over a general area of 50 square kilometers.

We had our first taste of antelope meat that evening and I was introduced to our new guide, Mrude, a traditional doctor, originally from near the glacier source. 'Answering the call of the government that a doctor was needed at Jiri, my family and I moved here 16 years ago. But then, medicine is only my sideline. I still have to tend to the animals,' Mrude said.

While telling me about his background, he put some snuff tobacco from a goat horn container onto his thumbnail. Raising his thumb to his nose, he sniffed energetically. With each of these moves, he closed his eyes momentarily, as if in great contentment. Warren tried the snuff and closed his eyes too. But his face contorted and tears poured down his cheeks!

Digging one of the jeeps out of the mud

Our first taste of antelope

More digging, pushing and pulling

Meanwhile, Bumpy negotiated with the nomads to buy the stakes which held down their tents. Antelope horns, which have high medicinal value for the Chinese, were used by the Tibetans as tent stakes.

The next morning, we rose early and drove west toward Ganlong village, or the settlement near the glacier source. During the day, we crossed many streams. Mrude usually knew where the water was shallower. Nomads crossed these rivers all the time. Before driving across Garqu, a major tributary near the source, Dawa rolled up his trousers and tested the water depth; we were grateful that the Landcruisers' doors had tight seals! In the distance, we saw a huge glacier which was the source of the Garqu.

By mid-morning, we had left the tracks of the mining road and were, on and off, following some faint tracks, preserved by the frozen ground, from the 1976 and 1978 expeditions. At one point I saw a single well-used track. This bewildered me, as I was certain we were the first to bring a motorcycle into this area; at this point Warren was riding the bike between our two jeeps. In fact, as Mrude explained, the track had been left by the wild ass which always travel along the same route when they roam the area.

Dawa, meanwhile, found it difficult to suppress his smoking, which I had forbidden in the jeep. He began puffing on his cigarette with half his body leaning out of the window. He was taking my 'no-smoking-in-jeep' rule literally and didn't know I was really concerned about all the gasoline on top of the vehicle. Jokingly, I said: 'Smoke, if you don't exhale, or go ride in the third jeep.' Dawa turned his head around and looked at the huge expanse of land behind our trail. He never lit a cigarette in the jeep again!

After driving 45 kilometers, we were over the crest of a small hill, Juemoshan, by noon. As we were going downhill, even though the surface looked deceivingly hard, the jeeps got stuck in the mud over and over again. For the next four hours, we covered only six kilometers. The vehicles

Driving across Garqu

were also losing power because of high altitude and we were constantly in low gear and engaging the four-wheel drive. By now, everyone was so exhausted and demoralized that we decided to call it a day. We all needed a good rest to ensure further digging in the morning.

On the third day, we drove for a long time over the water of a small stream called Saoliqu. As we were nearing Lake Juemoqo, we began to get alarmed as our gasoline supplies were fast being depleted. Fortunately, the valley of the glacier source was in sight that evening. There I calculated that we had traveled 155 kilometers (including the free-spinning mileage when stuck) since leaving the main road and had been consuming roughly one liter of gas per kilometer (2.35 miles per gallon). More than half the gasoline was gone. As returning would take as much gas as going in, we tried not to think about how we would make it back to the road.

We set up our base camp at 5,200 meters next to two black nomadic tents. I was totally amazed that at such a forbidding altitude, Tibetan nomads lived here year round. To our east was a huge glacier which guarded the entrance to the valley. To the west we saw more glaciers in the distance. But the Jianggendiru glacier we were seeking was still nowhere in sight. Looking at our one-to-a-million scale topographic map, we consoled ourselves that it was only one centimeter away, at the southernmost end of the valley.

I type a report inside one of the dome tents

Over the next three days we explored the northern end of this valley, and befriended the nomads. Our Tibetan neighbors were extremely hospitable. A lamb was slaughtered to feed us. Rested, we arranged to hire a few yaks for the hike to the glacier source. Now we were about two kilometers east of the flowing Marqu, the name given by the local Tibetans to Tuotuohe, the glacier source of the Yangtze.

The baby yaks in their herd all had artificial horns. It turned out that the nomads attached these to the baby yaks' heads so that the mother yaks would be poked when their calves tried to suckle. The wooden horns were not taken off until after the nomads had successfully milked the yaks. The same method is used when the nomads want to wean the baby yaks in the fall.

The local Tibetans attach wooden horns to the baby yaks

On August 3, we left Bumpy and Shorty with the jeeps at base camp and proceeded to hike south inside the valley. We had four yaks, three for carrying our load and one for riding. There were five of us, Dawa and Mrude walked all the time. Warren, Jeff and I took turns riding the one white yak. For every hour of the journey, each of us would get to ride for 20 minutes.

'Would you like a sip of water?' Jeff asked from the yak as he offered his canteen. 'No thanks…I prefer…to drink…when riding', came my reply. At such high altitude, drinking, talking, or even chewing gum exerts so much strength that it disrupts the pattern of breath and thus affects the pace of hiking. I had to break up my sentences into small phrases, punctuated by heavy breathing. However, the person taking his turn on the yak would speak normally.

As each of us rode only 20 minutes at a time, our watches became the most frequently consulted instruments over the next two days. When it came to my turn to ride, there were two things on my mind. One was getting to the source. The other was devising a strategy so that next time we crossed the river, it would be my turn on the yak again — the river water was freezing cold for those who had to cross it on foot!

On the afternoon of August 4, the glacier source was finally in sight. Like the claws of a gigantic lobster, the two glaciers of Jianggendiru came down from the ice field into the valley. Melted water from the glaciers fed the Marqu which was considered the source of the Yangtze. We pitched our tent at the tongue of the longer glacier and, tired as we were, immediately began exploring the area. Two nomadic families were living within sight of this southernmost glacier.

Jeff rode the yak across the freezing water

As the river left the tongue of the 12.5-kilometer-long glacier, it was about two meters in width. The color of the freezing water was slightly whitish. But when I looked at it again the following day, it had turned clear. We collected some rock samples and took pictures.

In the evening, I chatted with Tibetans from the two nomadic tents. They told me about the geography of the area and how it suited their life-styles. They could not understand why I made such a big deal about their being the first family living along the Yangtze — to them nomadic tents were all the same. One young man sang us a song in Tibetan from a favorite legend before we retired to our own tent.

On August 5, I hiked up nearby hills and confirmed that rivers over the divide all flowed south toward Tibet and did not drain into the Yangtze system north of the mountain. Mrude took advantage of the free time and visited friends and relatives he hadn't seen for years.

On the morning of August 6, we took a risk and hiked inside the glacier, treading on ice. Walking upstream, we cautiously moved into a palace of sculpted ice, where the sun had a blinding effect. We stayed only long enough to take photographs and get some water samples. The source here flowed through a channel where the whole streambed was formed by ice. Even though I knew two teams had been here before us, it was indeed an exciting moment. It was like fairyland; with this huge ice palace around us, we became childlike, collecting the first rocks from the streambed as souvenirs.

We packed up camp by mid-morning and began hiking back to base. Descending and better acclimatized, we gained speed. Hiking in, we had to cut the days short to allow time for the yaks to graze. Going out, we had less mercy and pushed them on, since we knew they could graze continuously for the next month or so at home. We arrived at base camp at dusk.

Shorty and Bumpy were delighted to see us back so soon. They thought we would not be back for days. While we were gone, a blizzard hit them. Our group some 20 kilometers into the valley, knew nothing of it. The wind was so strong that the tents had been blown off the ground and Shorty and Bumpy had had to run after them. From this valuable experience, Shorty was able to conclude that dome tents roll away faster than square-bottomed ones! Now the tents, besides being staked more firmly, were tied to the jeeps with extra cords.

The next morning, we felt a bit sad as we bade farewell to our nomadic friends. Bumpy and Shorty had become very close friends with the nomad family while we were gone. I explained our gasoline crisis to Mrude and asked for the shortest possible way back. Mrude had no conception that the gasoline supply had any bearing on the distance we could cover. On the

We took it in turn to ride the yak

The two glaciers of Jianggendiru

Within one day the weather changes from this ...

other hand, I had no conception that such 'common sense' needed further explanation. I must have convinced him somehow, anyway, as the return trip only took us 91 kilometers and we were back at the Road Maintenance Station as night fell. In all that time, each jeep was stuck only once, compared to the countless times coming in. The earth had hardened in the few days we were at the glacier source. Winter at such an altitude comes very quickly.

We left the high plateau and went on to Xining, provincial capital of Qinghai Province. There I made arrangements for our final exploration of the Yangtze. Back in April, Yuan Genshen, a researcher at the Yangtze Valley Planning Office at Wuhan, revealed to me some important data regarding the headwaters of the Yangtze. Yuan was a key member on both the 1976 and 1978 expeditions to the source and had flown over the area on reconnaissance of the great river.

His figures revealed that the Dam Qu was a comparable source to Tuotuohe. It had almost five times the flow volume, and was similar in length. The Dam Qu source had never been properly explored. The Chinese had simply noted it to be near a peak, Xiariabashan, on the eastern Tanggula Range. At Xining, we began to plan for our trip to southeastern Qinghai to explore this disputable source of the Dam Qu.

Over dinner with the governor of Qinghai Province, Huang Jingpo, who helped us to get crucial logistical support on our way to the source, I learned that Yao Maoshu, the lone rafter coming down the Yangtze from the source, had had an accident. His capsized raft and other belongings were found along the bank of the river and Yao was presumed dead.

I was sad to hear the news, but not surprised. I had seen the dragon in rage; the prince who tried to take him on singlehandedly happened only in fairy tales. Yao had christened his raft 'Descendant of the Dragon' and now the dragon had reclaimed him.

... to this

From Xining we drove south, passing more high mountains and the headwaters of the Yellow River before arriving at Yushu. From Tuotuohe to Yushu, the Yangtze travels 1,710 kilometers through the high plateau. Beyond Yushu, a series of drops begins. With its name changed to the Jinshajiang, it defines the provincial border of Sichuan and Tibet Autonomous Region.

We continued 200 kilometers west of Yushu to the town of Zadoi. The roads were getting worse all the time, so were our Landcruisers. Both vehicles began coughing badly. For a while, I thought they had caught pneumonia from Warren who was suffering from it! It turned out to be impurities in the gasoline clotting the fuel filters. On the way to Zadoi, it got so bad that we had to stop every ten kilometers to clean out the filters. By now, we had become very intimate with these two vehicles. Shorty thought the Landcruisers would have had a more comfortable life if they had been sold to someone else, rather than to us. I couldn't have agreed more.

The town of Yushu

The upper Lancang (Mekong) River flows outside the town of Zadoi. To the west, the source of Dam Qu lies about a week away on horseback in a marshland some 4,500 meters high. I had hoped to spend my 36th birthday at the source. But it was not to be. The nomads who owned the horses we needed were not very cooperative. We spent a quiet evening at Zadoi on August 26, but with one little surprise. Jeff produced two cans of shark-fin soup for a birthday celebration.

Three frustrating days were spent procuring the 12 horses we needed. Everybody was getting noticeably tired. Government officials explained the difficulties they faced. Following decentralization and the break up of the communes, all livestock was returned to the individual and the government had problems getting even a few horses. They could no longer make the nomads comply with their wishes.

On August 30, we finally got our 12 horses together. But the saddles and stirrups had to be rented, some here, some there, from many different households. With our two new Tibetan interpreters and two guides, we left Zadoi, heading west.

We rode for four days

For four days we rode up mountains, through plush green valleys, in rain, hail and, at times, snow. The fast-approaching winter took what little air we had left out of us. Along the way, I spoke with many nomads who had roamed the area in search of pastures for their herds. Soon, a geography of the area became apparent, which contradicted what I had previously read about the source of the Dam Qu. Everyone spoke with certainty that the Dam Qu did not originate from Xiariabashan, but began in a high marshland only four days west of Zadoi. Xiariabashan was still farther west, about seven days away.

Shorty was no horseman; he was sick and tired of falling off. Bumpy was bored, and was constantly taking target practice shots at the marmots; fortunately for the marmots, he was a lousy shot. Warren got dizzier and sicker by the day, while Jeff, a man of few words, began mumbling to himself. Even the horses were homesick; our guides spent an entire day retrieving three that tried to run home. The only thing that kept my spirits up was the old proverb: 'When drinking water, think of the source.' I was determined not just to think about the source, but to drink from it, too.

On the fourth day, we arrived at a high mountain marshland basin called Kaxigong. Around it were many undulating hills and the snowcapped peaks of the Tanggula Range rose in the distance to the south. We were told

The marshland basin of Kaxigong

that the river meandering through the basin formed by these hills was one of the headwaters of Dam Qu, and the source was near the top of a saddle-shaped hill to the northeast of the basin. We set up camp among other nomad tents. If indeed the nomads were right, we had made a very important discovery — a newer and longer source of the Yangtze. Our new discovery added approximately 60 kilometers to the length speculated by the Chinese team. This meant the Dam Qu was a much more important source than Tuotuohe.

I spoke at great length with some of the most experienced nomads of Kaxigong, trying to pinpoint exactly where we were on the map. The basin falls at 32.7 N, 94.6 E and at 4,500 meters, as far as we could ascertain. They pointed out that the actual source was approximately five kilometers further, at a watershed on a hill called Jari. To the other side of this saddle-shaped hill, all water drained toward the Jaqu, a tributary of the upper Lancang River system. The stream, which originated from an underground marshland spring 20 meters from the top of Jari Hill, was called Guangzhugou by the nomads. This Guangzhugou, the Tibetans said, was the source of the Dam Qu.

With the help of the local nomads, I began drawing sketch maps of the region, trying to identify hills, rivers and valleys by their Tibetan names, to help future explorers relocate the site. We explored some of the tributaries to verify that the Guangzhugou was indeed the longest tributary. Another important source, Shaja, originating from a hill called Wolak ten kilometers to the southeast of Kaxigong, was also explored.

On September 3, with our Tibetan guide Bumai and Jeff, I followed the Dam Qu toward Jari Hill on horseback. The sky was grayish-black. It had been half hailing and half snowing since we left camp. As the altitude rose, the temperature dropped. We rode for 90 minutes through marshes; all the while, many thoughts flooded my mind. We were approaching the Yangtze water at its purest; the water was becoming more and more sacred with every step. I took great care not to disturb the water, as I felt a connection to the 300 million people living downriver, all of whom would be familiar with the famous proverb. I finally arrived at a hole oozing water from the ground. It was 13:44 hours on September 3, 1985.

I dismounted in front of the spring. Without saying a word, I fell to my knees. Using my two hands, I scooped up some water to my mouth. Jeff kept our video machine rolling. He wanted to record that moment of satisfaction on my face. There was one thing he could not have captured:

the water was freezing; but it warmed my heart.

The source

Wuhu is a city in Anhui Province along the lower Yangtze. As one of the four major rice markets of China, the port is busy with boats and barges of all sizes. This stretch of the river is also home to the endangered Yangtze alligator.

The Nanjing Bridge serves both rail and automobile traffic. The approach span on the northern bank connects the four-lane road bridge above with that of the double-track railway bridge below. Very long approaches are necessary in order to give enough clearance to allow the passage of 10,000-ton ships. Consequently the total length of the bridge is nearly seven kilometers.

Preceding pages and above
The pipelines of the oil refinery at Jiujiang connect the petro-chemical plant to tankers docking nearby. Oil is a major export which earns the country its much needed foreign currency.

Right
The towering furnaces of the Wuhan Iron and Steel Company dominate the skyline.

The Wuhan steel mill, one of the country's largest, was first constructed in 1957, and presently employs over 120,000 workers. It has a complete production system composed of mining, ore dressing, refractory material, coking, sintering, iron-making, steel-smelting and steel-rolling.

A woman welder at a shipyard by the bank of the Yangtze below Jiujiang. Small operations like this one construct ships and barges up to a couple of hundred tons and help to maintain the boats as well.

Right
Shipbuilders working on the hull of a ship at Wuhan. Here ships of much larger tonnage can be built.

Signs and people crowd the streets of Wuhan, provincial capital and largest city of Hubei Province. An array of advertisement signs compete for attention with political banners.

*A child living along the Yangtze poses for a portrait
with his navy hat.*

Following blasting of the matchlock cannons at Honghu, duck-hunters in small boats chase after the injured mudhens with long spears.

Left
Fishing village along the lakefront of Honghu, a lake which drains into the Yangtze in Hubei Province.

Fishing families living along Lake Honghu. While all families have fixed homes in villages along the lake, many still live on boats during certain months of the year when fishing and duck-hunting are in season.

Following pages
The Gezhouba Dam at Yichang is the first dam built on the main stem of the Yangtze River. It generates 14 billion kilowatt-hours of electricity annually and improves navigation inside the Three Gorges.

Preceding pages
Of the three shiplocks at Gezhouba Dam, two are 280 meters long and 34 meters wide with a minimum depth of five meters at the sill. These are the largest locks in China and can allow passage of ships up to 10,000 tons.

The sun setting inside the Three Gorges at Zigui, a town on the northern bank of the Yangtze. If a second dam at Sandouping were to be constructed, many such towns would be flooded.

North of Zigui is the 3,053-meter-high peak Dashenlongjia, home of the legendary Wild Man of Hubei. Here, birch trees take on the look of a forest in flames.

*Fishermen repair their nets near Badong, a city
inside the Three Gorges.*

An old lady at the village of Meirendao inside the Three Gorges.

Within the gorges, fishermen using hand-held nets catch fish sometimes weighing many kilos. Some are taken to the local markets while others are sold to people on boats going up and down the river.

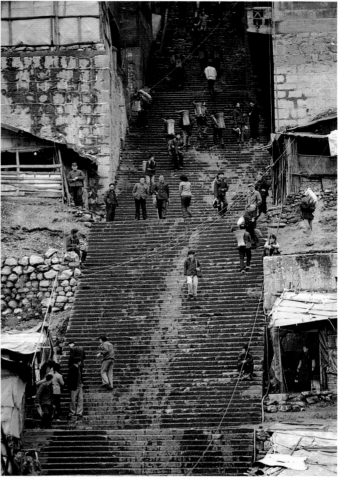

Long stairways lead up from the river's bank to the Badong streets. With the fluctuation of high and low waters during wet and dry seasons, houses within the Gorges have to be built high up the bank.

Left
Barges dock at Badong to load cargo before being towed downriver.

Left
Markings up the cliff-side show that the river level can vary by as much as 40 meters.

Near Baidicheng, the Yangtze narrows into the Three Gorges. Precarious footpaths lining the cliff-sides offer the only land passage along this stretch.

Boats and barges dock at Wanxian at the upper end of the Three Gorges.

Right
Workers with heavy loads of coal on their backs hike along some switchbacks up the bank between Zigui and Badong.

A cable-tram takes people from the pier and ferry-crossing at Chongqing up to street level. The Yangtze here can swell to four times its original volume, with the level rising up to 40 meters. Chongqing is at the confluence of the Jialing River and the Yangtze.

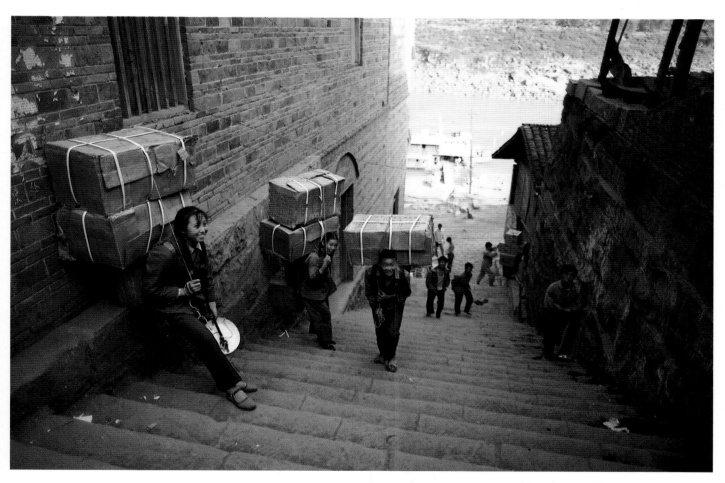

Long staircases are common sights along the Yangtze. Where there are no mechanical means to help in their ascent or descent, people have to bear huge loads between the waterfront below and the streets above.

Many markets line the banks of the Yangtze. They demonstrate China's free economy, burgeoning since the early 1980s.

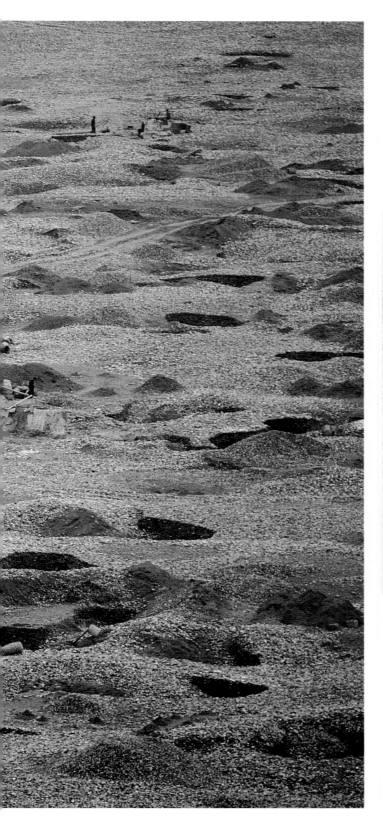

Chongqing farmers clear rocks and pebbles washed down by the flooding river. Temporary quarters are built to house these seasonal workers who sort out the rocks to be used later in the construction of buildings.

A fisherman near Hejiang is aided by his river otters. Rewarded with smaller fish, the otter is kept on a leash as it dives after bigger fish.

Rafters steer huge bamboo rafts that will be disassembled and sold in markets at the lower reaches.

*The Hanging Coffins of Gongxian in southern
Sichuan are the only remains of the Bo people who
once roamed this area. Records of this minority
tribe ended in the Ming Dynasty almost 400 years
ago. How and why these coffins were put on such
precipitous cliffs still baffles scholars today.*

The Yangtze is navigable from Shanghai to Xinshizhen in Sichuan—a distance of over 3,000 kilometers. Ships have to keep a constant vigil as they sail up the dangerous last 50-kilometer stretch from Pingshan to Xinshizhen. Beyond, the many rapids inside the gorges make the Yangtze increasingly hazardous.

Left top two
The Yi people of Liangshan in southern Sichuan are a minority nationality governed under a caste system which divides them into the Black Yi, or nobles, and the White Yi, or commoners. Two additional castes, the Ajia and Yaxi, are little more than slaves.

Above and near left
The Miao people of Sichuan live in the southern region of the province in the vicinity of Matongba, site of the Hanging Coffins.

Far left
A Han lady living in Meirendao, a village within the Three Gorges.

Similar colors to these on a wooden saddle are
applied by the Yi people to many other utensils such
as bowls, wine vessels and serving tables.

Right
Yi ladies hold an important place in society. With
interminable tribal feuds and the death of huge
numbers of warriors, the only chance of a peaceful
settlement was often for women to step in and
arbitrate.

*Sections of the River of Golden Sand (Jinshajiang),
a name given to the Upper Yangtze above Yibin, form
the provincial demarcation between Yunnan and
Sichuan. Here on the hills of Qiaojia a ferry crossing
links roads in northeastern Yunnan with those of
southern Sichuan.*

Run-off water during the rainy season cuts deep grooves into the hills. These canyons and gorges in northeastern Yunnan near Qiaojia contain many tributaries which drain into the Yangtze. Desparately short of fertile land, any flat tracts are transformed into arable land on this eastern end of the plateau.

Because of the high mountains and deep gorges, road construction is no easy task in this part of China. Extensive surveying is necessary before a new road can be planned and built.

Left
In drier regions near Butuo County, southern Sichuan, the Yi maintain their hillside plots by labor-intensive farming. Some of these areas yield little besides corn, potatoes and barley.

A Yi woman of Liangshan, in her traditional headdress and wig, smiles shyly for a portrait.

Left
Near Qiaojia where the Yangtze defines the border between Yunnan and Sichuan, the river takes on a golden tint from the setting sun, as if trying to live up to its name, the River of Golden Sand.

Left
Narrow paths are carved out of the mountainside along the gorges of the upper Yangtze. Here at Tiger Leaping Gorge in northwestern Yunnan, a mule caravan proceeds cautiously along the precipitous cliff toward a tungsten mine 4,000 meters up the mountain.

The Yangtze River cuts a deep gorge along its path in northwestern Yunnan. The Tiger Leaping Gorge is famed for its tremendous drop, 210 meters within a 17-kilometer stretch. On both sides the Yulong Snow Range and the Harba Snow Mountain rise over 5,000 meters in altitude, making the gorge one of the deepest in the world.

At Lijiang in northwestern Yunnan, one member of
a traditional Naxi orchestra plays an instrument
resembling the Chinese pipa.

Right
The town of Lijiang is the historical home of the Naxi
people, an ethnic minority in Yunnan Province with
a population of about a quarter-million.

The Yi people smoke a locally grown tobacco called Lanhuayan. The gracious skirts of the women are considered so sacred that it is taboo for a man to touch one.

Right
Lake Luguhu of Yongling, bordering Sichuan and Yunnan, is home to the Moso, a sub-group of the Naxi. Here lives a community which still adheres to its traditional matrilineal society.

For the Moso who live on the plain of Yongling, the women within a household reign over the family fortune and family names are passed down from mothers to daughters.

Following pages
A high mountain lake in the Tibetan region of northwestern Yunnan between the Mekong and Yangtze divide. Here the alpine forest begins as pine, then becomes fir and juniper as the altitude rises. At 3,800 meters, many varieties of rhododendron grow near a logging camp at Zhongdian.

At a Tibetan festival on the Zhongdian plateau of Yunnan, men and women come in their best costumes and participate in contests of horsemanship, tug-of-war, dances and even a game of mahjong.

Across the border of Yunnan in Tibet is the small town of Yanjing (Brine Well). Here terraces built along the Mekong serve as drying decks for salt water produced from wells sunk into the river. As the salt is collected, it is weighed and put in yak-hair sacks to be transported into the Tibetan interior on pack animals.

Markam (Gartog) in southeastern Tibet is only 50 kilometers west of the Yangtze. Here the Khampa Tibetans wear colorful boots and adorn their much treasured horses with elaborate stirrups and horse-blankets.

At Litang east of the Yangtze in western Sichuan, nomadic Tibetans of the Washi tribe adorn their heads with silver bowl-like ornaments. The hair of the women is braided into 108 plaits and more jewelry and ornaments are attached.

Right
At the confluence of the Batang River and the Yangtze, Tibetan villages are scattered along the banks. The scaffolding along the sides of the houses is used for drying grains.

Following pages
Standing facing each other, Tibetan men and women of the Washi tribe near Litang perform a popular dance called the 'Guo Zhuang,' during their summer horse-race gathering.

A pair of yaks plow the field on the plateau near Riwoqe in northeastern Tibet. In some areas, because of the short growing season, the soil has to be turned following harvest and before the bitter wind sets in.

Right
While most of Tibet is nomadic, populations are centered around the few pastoral regions relatively lower in altitude and slightly more conducive to marginal farming. In these areas, Tibetans live in permanent houses.

Along the road that crosses northern Tibet, a lone Buddhist devotee lives in an isolated tent and spends long hours every day carving votive inscriptions and images onto rocks as a meritorious act.

Right
The Potala Palace on the Red Hill dominates Lhasa. As the historical residence of the Dalai Lama, the fortress-like structure epitomizes the traditional architecture of the Tibetans. It is said that the Potala, which served as the winter palace for the spiritual leader, has 1,000 rooms. Today it is maintained as a museum for visitors to the high plateau.

These Tibetans maintain a nomadic lifestyle, grazing their livestock near the headwaters of Tuotuohe. Glacial peaks of the Tanggula Range form a back-drop to grazing horses of the Jiri nomads, gathering here for their annual horse-racing event. At such a remote and sparsely populated location, even a congregation of 40 to 50 people is considered a large group.

Above
Summer at an altitude of over 4,500 meters can be deceiving. Morning frost is almost a daily occurrence and horses have to be covered with blankets despite the gleaming sun. The peak in the background is that of Geladandong, looking from the northeast. The glaciers of its western foothills are considered the source of the Tuotuohe.

At the valley where the glacial source of the Yangtze is located, nomads live in black yak-hair tents and tend to their sheep and yak herds. In the background is one of the glaciers which guards the entrance to this valley. Wild yaks roam this area and their gigantic horns are used by the nomads as containers for the milk gathered from their yaks or sheep. Sling shots made of yak or sheep wool are used to propel stones and control the herd.

As one of two nomadic families living near the tongue of Jianggendiru Glacier, this husband, wife and son were considered the first family to be living along the Yangtze until further exploration proved otherwise.

Right
A flock of sheep graze at the confluence of two headwaters, both fed by the glaciers of Geladandong Peak. The group of white animals in the distance are sheep, the black animals are yak.

Pages 144-5
A flock of sheep grazing at the entrance of the glacial valley. The glacier in the background is one of many that feed water into upper Tuotuohe, known as Marqu by the local Tibetans.

Preceding pages
Melting water from Jianggendiru Glacier cuts through the tongue of the glacier at the southern end of the valley in the form of an ice channel and becomes the Tuotuohe. From 1976 until our expedition in 1985, this was considered the source of the Yangtze. We discovered a longer source at Dam Qu.

Hidden in the hills north of Yushu, a monastery
celebrates a three-day festival with religious dramas.
Tibetans converge to observe the spectacular event
presented by monks dressed in elaborate costumes and
spiritual masks who perform to the accompaniment
of music.

At Kaxigong near the headwaters of Dam Qu and the newly discovered source of the Yangtze, Tibetan nomads, young and old, converge for a religious event on the grassland. Despite the sun, summer clothing remains heavy. The high winds and ultra-violet light on the plateau also make the wearing of goggles popular among the nomads.

EPILOGUE

It has been almost three years since I finished my expedition to the Yangtze. China, as can be expected from a nation fast trying to modernize, has changed a lot. On the other hand, being one of the oldest and most enduring civilizations in the world, a lot will never change.

Since 1986, a couple of Western groups have entered the regions of the upper Yangtze and two sizable Chinese teams have rafted down the Yangtze, thus achieving the aim of Yao Maoshu. I'm glad that more attention is being given to such a great river and hope that this will help people better understand the world we live in.

In January 1986, I published a preliminary report on the discovery of the new source of the Yangtze River in *Geographic Knowledge*, a publication of the Geographic Institute of Academia Sinica. Later that year, the Chinese press also reported that the Dam Qu should be considered the official source of the Yangtze River.

I have altered the sequence of events at times, in the book, to give cohesiveness. Many people, who were vital to the success of the expedition but whose involvement or contribution was relatively short, have not been mentioned in the text.

I have written this book as an account of our group's contribution to geographic discovery and in the hope that it will inspire others to advance this knowledge in the future.

Pages 154-5
Jari Hill is the divide between Dam Qu and the Mekong. On one side flowing westward is the source of Dam Qu, and on the other flowing eastward is the tributary of the upper Mekong, shown here between Kaxigong and Zadoi.

Pages 156-7
The upper Dam Qu, coming down Jari Hill from its source, meanders through the Kaxigong basin, and flows past small nomadic camps. A few kilometers from this site, eastward and upriver, is the newly established source of the Yangtze.

APPENDIX

Upper Yangtze Expedition Logistics:
(prepared in 1984)

I Highest Road Point at Tuotuoheyan to Source of River by Land

Under usual conditions, when the road in southern Qinghai is 'ideal', a drive from Golmud (3,200 m) to Tuotuoheyan (4,533 m) can be covered in 2 days, a distance of approximately 415 km. (Fenghuoshan, 320 km south of Golmud, is the most treacherous section of this road.)

From Tuotuoheyan, if explorations are to be launched to the source of the Yangtze, a minimum of 2 weeks turn around time has to be put aside. In 1976, the Chinese team, with full land support, started off from Wenquan (Hotspring) south of Tuotuoheyan at approximately 125 km north of Tanggula Shankou at 5,300 m. The Chinese team left Wenquan by an unpaved road west of the Golmud–Lhasa Highway. They drove for 5 days trying to cover the 160 km to the banks of Tuotuohe. The first day they covered only 7 km with a full day's driving. On the fifth day they reached Tuotuohe where they set up camp at 5,500 m. Two more days and 40 km by horse took the team to the glacier source. The average temperature from June to September at this point is calculated to be around 3°C. Tuotuohe from the source to the confluence of the Dam Qu is 375 km, to the confluence with Qumar is 660 km. This region holds an average of 1 person per 10 square km.

II River Condition from Source to First Road Point at Tuotuoheyan and beyond to Confluence of Dam Qu

The source of Tuotuohe develops from a glacier on the southwestern side of the 6,621 m-high peak, Geladandong, (meaning high and long peak in Tibetan). In this area there are over 20 peaks rising to 6,000 m and over 40 glaciers. Also feeding the river at this point is a glacier of Peak Miqianggendiyr (6,548 m). This glacier is 12.5 km long and 1.6 km wide. The river first flows north through a canyon 15 km long and 3 km wide. The riverbed width here is 1.5 km. For a while the river divides into 2 then joins. The river width here is between 4 to 6 m and flows at 0.6 m per second. On both sides of this canyon are 5 small glaciers and 20 more streams from other glaciers. The altitude here is 5,300 m.

Near the exit of this canyon, the riverbed cuts suddenly downward, thus forming another small canyon 5 to 6 km long. The banks here on both sides are 20 m high. Once outside these mountains the river enters into an expanse of plait-like streams 20 km north–south, 7 km east–west. Sandbars are common, especially during drier seasons. Beyond, the river continues north cutting through the low hills of Dzorgan-Ula Shan forming a 30 km-long, 1 km-wide river canyon. The banks here are sloping and are at a height of between 4 to 9 m above the river. The northward flow ends at Lake Huhuhu where it turns east. From the source to this lake is a distance of 131 km.

Where the river meets the Golmud–Lhasa Highway at Tuotuoheyan, it widens to approximately 270 m. The bridge spanning the river is 273 m long. There are more sandbars here during dry seasons and the river is 3 m at the deepest, flows at 2 m per second, has an average annual flow of 29.1 sq m per second and an annual total flow of 920 million cubic m.

Near Nagjibalong (58 km east of the highway), the Dam Qu flows in from the southern bank. At this point, both banks are hills forming a canyon 200 m wide. The river width is 30 m and the northern shore is a 12-m-high cliff. This point is considered the end of Tuotuohe and below is considered Tongtianhe. From the source to here is 375 km. Every year from October to May, the river freezes over. Lowest temperature is –42°C. At this altitude there is a layer of permaforst 1 m underground that is inpenetrable to meltwater and thus keeps the topsoil moist. This had made the passage of vehicles on roads that are unpaved extremely difficult.

III River from Confluence of Dam Qu to Yushu (This Part Is Called Tongtianhe)

The first county town Tongtianhe comes to is Qumarleb (Chu-ma-lai). Here the river is flat and wide and slow-flowing. Beyond, it begins to meander between hills. The lower stretch of Tongtianhe begins from Gongsangzhi then goes through Anzhong to Chumda, 26 km east of Yushu (3,700 m). Agricultural land flanks both sides of the river. A bridge crosses the river at Chumda. The road from Tuotuoheyan going through Golmud, then south before Xining and through Madoi to Yushu is 1,832 km. This distance can be covered in 5 to 6 days, granted the passage between Tuotuoheyan to Golmud is smooth going.

At Chumda, the river level is 3,700 m. Tongtianhe (from the confluence of Dam Qu to Chumda) accounts for an approximate drop of 800 m in 813 km. The river from the source to Yushu is 1,188 km.

IV River from Yushu in Qinghai to Yibin of Sichuan

This part of the Yangtze is called the Jinshajiang (River of Golden Sand). The river length is 2,308 km from Yushu to Yibin. South of Dege, the river is between 100 and 200 m wide. The mountains on both sides of the canyon often rise 3,000 m above the river. Between Yushu and Batang, a distance of 640 km, the river drops 1,400 m, averaging 2 m per km.

The Jinshajiang defines the provincial border between Sichuan and Tibet. Along this stretch, Tibetans operate ferrying services at different points using yak-skin coracles.

Dege is 25 km east of the river, on the convoy road from Chengdu to Lhasa. A bridge crosses the Yangtze at Gamtog. From Yushu by road, through Serxu, south to Maniganggo, then west to Dege is 481 km. This can be covered in 2 days. The road from Maniganggo to Dege goes through the Cho La Pass at 4,600 m.

The river at Dege is 200 m wide and flows swiftly. What took Tibetan yak caravans 3 days to cover in the past can now be achieved in 4 hours by boat.

From Dege to Batang by road is 845 km going through Maniganggo again, then south through Garze, Dawu, Yajiang and Litang. This can take between 3 to 4 days. Chubalong by the river is 32 km west of Batang, a bridge spans the Jinsha here.

The distance between Batang and Shigu in Yunnan is 369 km and the river drops 877 m. At Shigu, the Jinsha makes a 180° turn and flows north. 35 km below Shigu, but north of Shigu in direction, the river flows into Tiger Leaping Gorge. Shigu to Yibin is a total of 800 km of navigable stretches.

Qiaotou is at the lower entrance of Tiger Leaping Gorge. From Batang to here, through Markam, Yanjing, Deqen and Zhongdian, is 612 km. This can be covered in 2 days. (The section of the road between Markam and Deqen can be closed, by landslides in summer and by snow in early fall through winter. If this happens, the road from Batang, back east to Litang, Xiangcheng and Zhongdian, to Qiaotou which is 634 km long is used.)

Where the Hutiaojiang (Tiger Leaping River) flows into the Jinshajiang is an entrance into the Tiger Leaping Gorge. Within the next 12 km inside the gorge, the river drops from 1,800 m to 1,630 m, in a series of 7 falls. At the narrowest point the river is merely 30 m wide and, on both sides, the mountains rise to around 5,000 m (5,596 m for the Yulongxueshan to the east and around 4,700 m for the Harbaxueshan to the west). The gorge created by the river is over 3,000 m deep. A hazardous footpath goes into the gorge along the west bank of the river. Inside the gorge the widest part of the river is only 60–80 m depending on the time of the year.

At Sanjiangkou the Jinshajiang makes another 180° turn and flows south. From the northern exit of Tiger Leaping Gorge to Gili is only 36 km as the crow flies, but the river distance is 230 km between the 2 points. There is a drop in elevation of over 500 m.

At Jinjianjia the river makes a 90° turn eastward. Here the river width is 100–250 m.

From Yunnan's Zhongjiang (east of Heqing) to Sichuan's Xinshizhen, within a river distance of over 900 km, there are over 400 large rapids. Particularly famous is the Laojuntan (above Puduhe, which flows into Dian Chi of Kunming), the rapid is 4 km long with a drop of over 50 m. Here the waves are particularly high and the undercurrent extremely great. At points where a ferry plies the opposite bank, the boat has to travel upriver several km before coming down to reach the same point across the river. In the past, only the 62-km section from Pingshan to Yibin was navigable. But today, river traffic is possible from Yibin to Xinshizhen, a total of 120 km.

Along this lower stretch of the Jinshajiang, beyond Qiaotou, is Sudiqiao. (The bridge 46 km east of Lijiang was washed away in November 1981 when I was last there.) From Qiaotou to this bridge through Lijiang is 146 km. Next road point is at the bridge of Jinjiang 189 km south through Yongsheng. From here to Dukou is 212 km through Huaping. Dukou is a sizable industrial city and the Yalong Jiang with more water than the Yellow River adds 50 percent more water to the Jinsha. Beyond Dukou the road to Kunming is 1,169 km.

V Conclusion

	Distance (km)	Altitude (m)	Drop (m)
Source – Tuotuoheyan	317	5,500–4,533	967
Tuotuoheyan – Batangkou	871	4,533–3,700	833
Batangkou – Batang	640	3,700–2,700	1,000
Batang – Shigu	369	2,700–1,800	900
Shigu – Pingshan	1,237	1,800–279	1,521
Pingshan – Yibin	62	279–243	36
Total	3,496	—	5,257

The total length of the Yangtze from the source to Yibin is 3,496 km. Below Yibin, the Yangtze is 2,884 km long making a total river length of 6,380 km.

River Gradient from Tuotuoheyan to Yibin (Imperial system)

Begin	Elevation Stop	Difference	River Segment	Miles Total	Gradient (ft/mi)
14,500	14,000	500	123.3	—	4.1
14,000	13,000	1,000	171.1	294.4	5.8
13,000	12,000	1,000	177.1	471.5	5.6
12,000	11,000	1,000	168.6	640.1	5.9
11,000	9,000	2,000	98.8	738.9	20.3
9,000	7,000	2,000	190.6	929.5	10.5
7,000	5,000	2,000	186.3	1,115.8	10.7
5,000	3,000	2,000	303.2	1,419.0	6.6
3,000	1,000	2,000	110.5	1,529.5	18.1
1,000	800	200	201.1	1,730.6	1.1
Total	—	13,700 ft	1,730.6 mi	—	88.7 mi/average ft

Map reference, see page 164

Enlarged detail,
see page 165

NASA S/N 01   01

The Large Format Camera (LFC) is a
high-precision optical instrument which
flew on Mission 41-G of the Space
Shuttle Challenger in October 1984.
It provides distortion-free high-quality
(ten-meter resolution) images of the
earth taken from 228 kilometers above.
These high-resolution photographs can
be enlarged ten times or more with
little loss of image quality. In most
cases, the photographs are useable for
mapping applications at scales up to
1:50,000.

I was able to utilize these images in
planning, execution as well as verifica-
tion of my exploration work to the
source of the Yangtze. The image
shown here is a contact print of a three-
frame scene, covering an area of 170
km x 340 km, equivalent to 1:750,000
in scale.

On the left of the image is the trunk
river of Tongtianhe, downriver from
the confluence of Tuotuohe and Dam
Qu. The lower right of the image shows
the basin of Kaxigong just on the edge
of cloud cover (refer to enlargement of
this section on following page). This
basin is where the two headwaters,
Shaja and Guangzhugou, join together
becoming the Dam Qu. Since
Guangzhugou is the longer of the two
tributaries, it is thus considered the
source of the Yangtze.

282   07   19 02.3 12 4107 0822   282   07   19 02.3 12

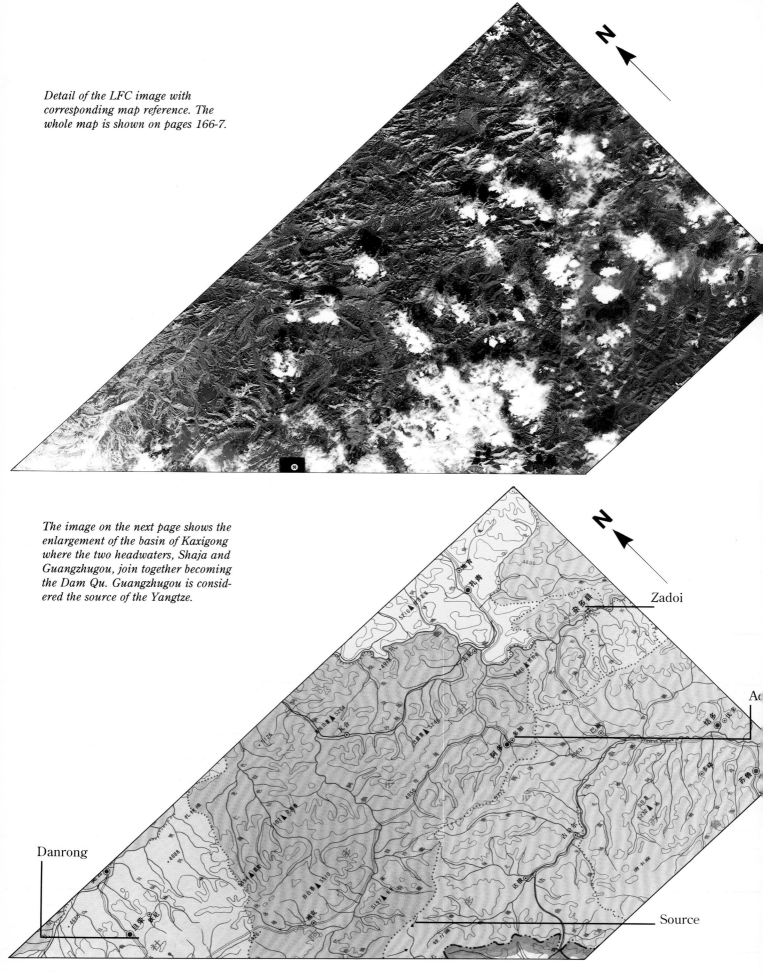

Detail of the LFC image with corresponding map reference. The whole map is shown on pages 166-7.

The image on the next page shows the enlargement of the basin of Kaxigong where the two headwaters, Shaja and Guangzhugou, join together becoming the Dam Qu. Guangzhugou is considered the source of the Yangtze.

Zadoi

Danrong

Source

N

龙毛涌
扎拉涌
莫云
齐荣
·4685 马
·4888
Danrong
旦荣
跃尼
扎拉涌
社
5394 ▲ 瞻爱
扎日娃 ▲ 5346
旦谷
日白赛
下 龙
坎各涌
5026·
·4742
当涌
浦克
Dam Qu
多忙涌
4996 ▲ 加老
当涌
巴庆
当涌
阿
靖尔娃
·4907
·4820
4901 ▲ 吉日日纠
Dam Qu
Guangzh
Dam Qu
结
5158 ▲ 港布古
·5124
阿日西诺 ▲ 5339
TIBI

This section of a map of Zadoi County was critical to us in locating the source of Dam Qu. Though names of rivers and streams are written in Chinese, they are phonetic transliterations of local Tibetan names. The upper arrow pinpoints the source of Dam Qu, a stream by the name of Guangzhugou. Below is Shaja, a slightly shorter tributary of Dam Qu. The basin situated to the east of the two streams is Kaxigong. The hill to the east of Guangzhugou, or the divide between the Mekong and the Yangtze, is called Jari.

INDEX